Pilgrim's Guide
to
Oberammergau

and its Passion Play

Second Edition 2008

Michael Counsell

CANTERBURY
PRESS
Norwich

First published in 2008 by
The Canterbury Press Norwich
(a publishing imprint of Hymns Ancient and
Modern Limited, a registered charity)
13–17 Long Lane, London EC1A 9PN

www.scm-canterburypress.co.uk

British Library Cataloguing in Publication data
A catalogue record for this book is available
from the British Library

ISBN 978-1-85311-891-3

Typeset by Regent Typesetting, London
Printed and bound by CPI Bookmarque,
Croydon, CR0 4TD

Contents

Some other books by Michael Counsell:

All Through the Night (Canterbury Press and
Westminster John Knox Press)

Every Pilgrim's Guide to the Journeys of the Apostles
(Canterbury Press)

The Little Book of Heavenly Humour by Syd Little with
Chris Gidney and Michael Counsell (Canterbury Press)

Every Pilgrim's Guide to England's Holy Places
(Canterbury Press)

A Basic Bible Dictionary (Canterbury Press)

A Basic Christian Dictionary (Canterbury Press)

The Canterbury Preacher's Companion
(Annual publication by Canterbury Press)

Introduction

An enjoyable holiday can be spent at any time in the foothills of the Alps, called Bavaria in Germany or the Tyrol in Austria and Switzerland. But one very special place is the village of Oberammergau, southeast of Munich in Germany. There, every ten years, a Passion Play is performed, which re-enacts, on a vast open-air stage, the events of the last week of the life of Jesus of Nazareth. Oberammergau nestles in the valley of the River Ammer between the Bavarian mountains; the village is dominated by the Parish Church and the Passion Play Theatre.

The Oberammergau Passion Play

This book may whet the appetite of those who would like to see the Oberammergau Passion Play, and encourage them to make plans in good time. Almost all the tickets to the Play are bought up two years beforehand. Those who wish to see the Play in 2010 are strongly advised to book as soon as possible (see page 19). Half a million people will see the Oberammergau Passion Play, at one of 102 performances, each lasting about five hours, five times a week between 15 May and 3 October in that year. This book will also be a souvenir to take home, to meditate on and to share with your friends; and it may encourage tourists to visit Oberammergau in other years.

Mountains

Those who are attracted to visit Bavaria and the Tyrol are not only interested in the towns and cities. The natural beauty of the mountains, valleys and lakes repays those willing to take a gentle stroll through the countryside with constantly changing vistas of delightful scenery. Many of the mountains have a *Sesselbahn* (chairlift) or a *Seilbahn* (cabin cable car), some of which, as well as taking skiers to the tops of the ski runs in winter, will, in summer, take passengers to the beginning of walks along well-marked mountain footpaths, where the route can be chosen to be as strenuous or easy as the walker requires.

Lakes

The mountain valleys were carved into shape by the glaciers of the last ice age, each of which, when it retreated, left a moraine of stones across the valley floor at the furthest point to which it carried them. These often formed natural dams to the rivers that still flow down from the mountains, and in many places a lake mirrors the peaks of the mountains above.

Wild flowers

In the spring and summer the Alpine flowers grow in profusion, forming a carpet of colour across the mountains. There are so many species that an expert or a good book is needed to identify them. And in some places there are special gardens where every known species is grown. Even in winter the hardy Edelweiss can be found in sheltered spots among the snow. Visitors are asked not to pick the wild flowers, as it prevents others from enjoying them, and there is always a risk that a species might die out.

Maypoles

Many Bavarian villages have a blue and white maypole in the centre, with symbols of all the trades plied there, to inform passing youths what apprenticeships may be available. If it is taken down for repainting it may be stolen by a rival village, and can only be bought back at the cost of a large quantity of beer.

People

The friendliness of the people, in their *lederhosen* or *dirndl* dresses, and the thigh-slapping *Schuhplattler* dances; the ample and jolly welcome of the hostess in the restaurant, and the cheerful yodeller who entertains there, all add to the enjoyment. With luck, you may even hear the town's 'oompah band'. Everywhere in the region you will be greeted by total strangers with the phrase '*Grüss Gott*,' meaning roughly, 'Greetings in the name of God,' and will be expected to reply with the same words. There are hints at the end of this book about learning a few phrases of German for those who do not already speak it. The dialect farewell, '*Pfüat di Gott*' ('*Pfüat eich Gott*,' if you are being formal or speaking to more than one person), is even harder to translate but, like the English word 'Goodbye,' it means something like 'God be with you, protect you and guide you.'

Mountain-top experiences

Many people have said that they feel nearer to God in the mountains. Not literally, of course, for we know that heaven is not a place above the clouds, but the state of being with God, and God is everywhere. But in the pure mountain air the grandeur of what God has created can be seen, and the puny size of our best efforts in comparison. It helps us to see ourselves in perspective, and our total dependence on God's care. In the silence we can pray without distractions. It was no accident that it was on a high mountain that Jesus was transfigured before his disciples and they recognized him as the Son of God. Immediately afterwards, however, they had to descend from the mountains to the busy life of the plain, with a sick boy and an unbelieving crowd. Our 'mountain-top experiences' – even those that happen in a theatre, a concert hall or a library – can inspire and strengthen us to love our neighbours when we come back down to earth.

AUTHOR'S NOTES

Capital letters on the word 'Village' always refer to the village of Oberammergau in Bavaria; on the word 'Play' to the Passion Play enacted there every ten years, and on the word 'Theatre' to the *Passionspielhaus* where it is performed.

Bible passages are quoted from the New Revised Standard Version. The prayers are for personal or group use.

A selection of hymns is included which may be used in churches in Oberammergau, or in churches, hotels, or on a coach on the way to and from the Village.

The general information supplied – in particular the arrangements in the Village, opening/closing times and telephone numbers – has been carefully checked at the time of writing, but inevitably some details may vary from time to time.

The index at the end enables immediate reference to the sections required.

Acknowledgements

The author thanks the following for their help in the preparation of this guide: the German National Tourist Office in London; the Oberammergau Tourist Information Office; and also the people of the Village and those who minister at the two churches there.

PRACTICAL INFORMATION FOR VISITORS

The Passion Play

The Oberammergau Passion Play is performed every ten years; in 2010 it will be from 15 May to 3 October on Saturdays, Sundays, Tuesdays, Thursdays and Fridays, from 14.30 (2.30 p.m.) to 17.00 (5 p.m.) and from 20.00 (8 p.m.) to 22.30 (10.30 p.m.). On Sundays, Tuesdays and Thursdays, most tickets are only available as two-day packages, called 'arrangements', including accommodation for two nights; on Fridays there are one-day packages with accommodation for one night; and on Saturdays you can buy a ticket without accommodation; see page 19. Otherwise, tickets for the Passion Play are almost unobtainable except through tour operators who have bought and paid for them two years beforehand. In 2000 there were a million applications for half a million tickets. There are very few returns, so turning up in the Village and hoping to buy tickets there usually leads to frustration. Nevertheless it is a delightful place to visit in non-Play years.

The stage in the Passion Play Theatre

GENERAL INFORMATION FOR VISITORS TO GERMANY

General information can be obtained from the German National Tourist Office, PO Box 2695, London W1A 3TN, open Monday to Friday 10 a.m. to 4 p.m.
Tel. 020 7317 0908, Fax 020 7317 0917.
E-mail: gntoLon@d-z-t.com; Skype germany.tourism
Internet: www.germany-tourism.co.uk or
www.germany-tourism.de

Bavarian Tourism, www.bayern.by/en/index.html or
german-embassy.org.uk/Bavaria.html

German Embassy, 23 Belgrave Square, London SW1X 8PZ.

German Information Centre, 34 Belgrave Square, London SW1X 8QB. Tel. 020 7824 1300, Fax 020 7824 1449.
Internet: www.london.diplo.de

Most towns have a Tourist Information centre indicated with the international 'i' symbol.

Carry your passport at all times. Have valid travel insurance. British and EU passport holders do not need a visa. Adult travellers alone with children should contact the German Embassy in the UK in advance to find out what documentation is required.

EMERGENCIES

British Embassy, Wilhelmstraße 70, 10117 Berlin, Germany. Tel. +49 (0)30 20457-0, consular 20457-579. Office hours Mon.–Fri. 9 a.m. – 5.30 p.m.
Internet: www.britischebotschaft.de

British Consulate-General, Möhlstraße 5, D-81675 München, Germany. Telephone +49 (0)89 211090, Fax +49 (0)89 21109 166. Office hours Mon.–Fri. 8.30 a.m. – 12 noon; Mon.–Thu. 1 p.m. – 5 p.m.; Fri. 1 p.m. – 3.30 p.m.

Details of all British Representatives abroad and travel advice can be found on the internet at www.fco.gov.uk . For services for Britons overseas tel. 020 7008 0210; for travel advice tel. 0845 850 2829.

Note: double 's' in German is often written with an ß, so that Straße is pronounced Shtraasseh. The house number follows the street name.

Emergency services in Germany

Police, Fire Brigade, Emergency Ambulance and Medical Emergencies throughout Europe: phone 112, but you may not be answered by anyone who speaks English.
Ambulance: in less urgent situations call the local ambulance service, using the local telephone number from this book or the telephone directory. For Oberammergau numbers see page xviii.

The following sections are listed in alphabetical order:

Church opening hours

Most churches in Bavaria open from Monday to Saturday 9 a.m. to 5.30 p.m. On Sundays they are only open during services, when you are welcome to worship but it is discourteous to wander around.

Conversion table

From	To	Multiply by	
Inches	Centimetres	2.54	0.3937
Feet	Metres	0.3048	3.2808
Yards	Metres	0.9144	1.0936
Miles	Kilometres	1.6090	0.6214
Acres	Hectares	0.4057	2.4649
Gallons	Litres	4.5460	0.2200
Ounces	Grams	28.35	0.0353
Pounds	Grams	453.6	0.0022
Pounds	Kilograms	0.4536	2.2046
Tons	Tonnes	1.0160	0.9843
To	From		Multiply by

Distances are in kilometres (km); approximately 8 km = 5 miles; 1 km = 0.62 miles, 100 km = 62.14 miles.

Electrical equipment

Current is 220 volts AC; plug sockets are of the European two-pronged design, so a travel adaptor is necessary. Airlines require electrical equipment to be carried in hand luggage.

Finance

German banking hours are generally Monday to Friday 8.30 a.m. till 4 p.m., closing for lunch from 1 to 2.30; but there are local variations; see page xix for banks in Oberammergau. Banks are closed on Saturdays and Sundays.

Do not change currency anywhere except at banks or legitimate *Bureaux de Change*; you may be arrested if found to be carrying forged currency. You can change travellers' cheques in exchange bureaux, marked *Wechsel*, some but not all banks, major post offices and some hotels, but not in guest houses. Always keep a note of the numbers of your travellers' cheques in a separate place. You can also draw cash with Visa cards or MasterCards through machines outside certain banks; if the ATM or cash machine (*Geldautomat*) is inside, you can usually gain entrance by inserting your card in the slot by the door. It is advisable to buy a small amount of euros before setting out; there is no limit on the amount in notes that you can change back into sterling when you return.

Health

Vaccinations and inoculations are not normally necessary, but any medicines or other health needs that may be required should be taken with you. Travellers from the UK should obtain a copy of the booklet 'T7.1 Health advice for travellers' from major post offices in the UK, follow its advice, obtain a European Health Insurance Card, and keep it with their passport. Also carry your driving licence or NHS medical card. To obtain information on medical treatment ask your tour operator or the local information office to contact the Local Health Insurance Fund (*Allgemeine Ortskrankenkasse* or AOK) or any Substitute Health Insurance Fund (*Ersatzkasse*, *Betriebskrankenkassen* or *Innungskrankenkassen*, etc.)

Doctors' surgery hours in Germany are generally from 10 a.m. till 12 noon and 4 till 6 p.m., except for Wednesdays and the weekend; for urgent cases call the emergency service, using the local telephone number from this book (for Oberammergau see page xviii) or the telephone directory. If there is no time to see a doctor first, a patient's European Health Insurance Card should be shown to the hospital on admission.

Dispensing chemist shops or pharmacies (*Apotheke*) have a night opening rota displayed in the window, and a flashing green cross or a big red 'A' outside:

The mains water is drinkable, but if you have a delicate stomach you are advised to buy bottled water.

Language

More German people speak English than English people speak German; see the section in this book on 'Learn a phrase a day' (page 90).

Poste restante

Letters or packages marked *Postlagernd* will be kept at the main post office of the town for up to four weeks.

Railways

Deutsche Bahn UK, Suites 6/8, The Sanctuary, 23 Oakhill Grove, Surbiton, Surrey KT6 6DU. Tel. 08718 80 80 66 (8p/minute), Fax 08718 80 80 65.
Internet: www.bahn.co.uk
E-mail: sales@bahn.co.uk

Security

Although crime is no worse in Germany than elsewhere you are advised to keep handbags, cameras, travel documents and passports attached to your person so as not to leave them behind anywhere.

Shops

Shops in Germany are usually open Mondays to Fridays from 9 a.m. to 6.30 p.m., and in bigger cities until 8 p.m., but some shops close from about noon to 2 p.m. **N.B. On Saturdays smaller shops open from about 9 a.m. to 2 p.m., and larger stores from 9 a.m. to 4 p.m. Most shops are closed on Sundays.**

Sizes

(approximately corresponding sizes)

Ladies' outer clothing

Germany & Holland	UK	France & Belgium	Spain	Italy & Scandinavia	Japan	USA
34	8/30	38	40	36	7	6
36	10/32	40	42	38	9	8
38	12/34	42	44	40	11	10
40	14/36	44	46	42	13	12
42	16/38	46	48	44	15	14
44	18/40	48	50	46	17	16

Shoes

Europe	UK	Japan	USA women	USA men
36	3	22	4½	
37	4	23	5½	
38	5	24	6½	
39	6	25	7½	6½
40	7		8½	7½
41	8			8½
42	9			9½
43	10			10½

Men's outer clothing		Men's shirts	
Europe	*UK/USA*	*Europe*	*UK/USA*
46	36	36	14
48	38	37	14½
50	40	38	15
52	42	39	15½
54	44	40	16
56	46	41	16½
		42	17
		43	17½

Telephones

You can make local and long-distance calls from post offices and public call boxes. Most kiosks accept phone cards which you can purchase at any post office.

To telephone to the United Kingdom from Germany: dial 0044, then the full UK number without the first 'o'. If you have a telephone chargecard from BT (www.payphones.bt.com/callingcards/), or one of the other UK telephone companies, they will tell you a number to dial direct from Germany to an English telephone number at low rates, or, for a surcharge, to connect to an English-speaking operator, but it is better to do this from a public telephone than from a hotel. Find out from your mobile telephone operator how to use it in Germany and what the roaming charges are.

When telephoning to Germany from the United Kingdom, dial 0049, then omit the first 'o'. For Oberammergau telephone 08822 from Germany, 00498822 from the UK.

Temperatures

Temperatures are measured in degrees Celsius or Centigrade: 0°C = 32°F; 10°C = 50°F; 20°C = 68°F; 50°C = 122°F; 100°C = 212°F

Time

European time is one hour in advance of Britain.

Tipping and etiquette

Tipping in Germany is purely voluntary (up to 10% of the total bill). It means you are expressing your particular satisfaction with the service you've received. All you need to know on the subject of etiquette is to maintain an attitude of polite reserve, to use the polite '*Sie*' form of address if you speak German, and to shake hands when you greet someone.

INFORMATION FOR VISITORS TO OBERAMMERGAU

Telephone: dial 08822 from outside Oberammergau, Ettal, Unterammergau and Linderhof, or 00498822 from the UK.

Oberammergau Tourist Information Office, Oberammergau Tourismus, Ammergauer Haus, Eugen-Papst-Str. 9a, 82487 Oberammergau, Germany, open Monday to Friday 9 a.m. to 6 p.m., Saturday 9 a.m. to 12 noon. Tel. +49 (0) 8822 92 31-0, Fax 92 31-90. E-mail: info@oberammergau.de.

The Ammergauer Haus can give information on accommodation in non-Play years. The information leaflet available there gives addresses of doctors, dentists, etc.

Information on Oberammergau is also available on the internet, much of it in English, at www.oberammergau.de

---

EMERGENCIES IN OBERAMMERGAU

(Dial 08822 from outside Oberammergau, Ettal, Unterammergau and Linderhof.)
Police: Feldiglgasse 17. Tel. 945830; in emergencies phone 110
Fire: 112
Ambulance: 19222
Mountain rescue: 6333

The following sections are listed in alphabetical order:

Accommodation

In Play years, accommodation in the region is almost unobtainable except as part of a Play ticket booked in advance; at other times contact the *Verkehrsbüro* or travel office in each town for details of hotels and guest houses. The Campingpark, for tents or campervans, is at Ettalerstraße 56b, at the south of the Village near the entrance to the bypass road. Tel. +49 (0) 8822 94105, Fax 94197, www.campingpark-oberammergau.de

Banks in Oberammergau

Hypovereinsbank, Dorfstraße 3. Tel. 92900, open Mon.–Fri. 8.30 a.m. – 12 noon, 2 p.m. – 4 p.m., open till 5.30 p.m. on Thursday. Cash machine (*Geldautomat*) inside.

Kreissparkasse, Dorfstraße 23. Tel. 92040, open Mon.–Fri. 8.30 a.m. – 12 noon, 2 p.m. – 4 p.m., open till 5.30 p.m. on Thursday. Cash machine inside.

V-R Raiffeisenbank, Bahnhofstraße 24. Tel. 92110, open Mon.–Tue. 8 a.m. – 12 noon, 2 p.m. – 4 p.m.; Wed. 8 a.m. – 12 noon only; Thu. 8 a.m. – 12 noon, 2 p.m. – 5.30 p.m.; Fri. 8 a.m. – 4 p.m. Cash machine outside.

Don't arrive too late to reach the front of the queue at the bank before it closes at lunchtime or in the afternoon.

Bicycle hire

Sportcentrale Happistock, Bahnhoftstr, 6a. Tel. 4178; Radl Lang, Rottenbucher Str. 16. Tel. 1004.

Cabin cable car

From the WellenBerg swimming pool up the Laber (1,684 metres) to the mountain restaurant: 9 a.m. – 5 p.m. April–June and September–October; 9 a.m. – 6 p.m. July–August; 9 a.m. – 4.30 p.m. December–March. Tel. 4770.
E-mail: laber-bergbahn@t-online.de

Chair-lift

To the Kolbensattel (1,270 metres, mountain hut and snack bar at the summit): 9 a.m. – 4.45 p.m. in June–October and December–March. Tel. 4760.
E-mail: kolbensesselbahn@oberammergau.de

Chemist shops (see above, page xv)

Kofel-Apotheke, Ettalerstraße 12. Tel. 6664.
Sternapotheke, Dorfstraße 5. Tel. 3540 or 1000.

Climate

Bavaria is high, and temperatures can be colder than in Britain. Visitors to the Play will be sitting for long periods of time in the open air, so layers of warm clothing which can be added to or removed are recommended; also a waterproof coat and comfortable waterproof footwear. But bring sun-cream and head-covering too for swimming and sunbathing at the pool in Oberammergau, or elsewhere on your journey.

Getting there

Visitors in Play years can only spend one or at most two nights in or near Oberammergau, so most tours include a holiday in southern Germany or the countries around. Most visitors will come to the Village by coach, and be taken to their pre-booked accommodation in Oberammergau or the villages around, and brought to the Theatre by coach also. It is also possible to approach by car from Munich (München) along the A95 (E533) autobahn and then highway B2 towards Garmisch-Partenkirchen, but turning off at Oberau on to the B23 to Oberammergau; or by train from Munich changing at Murnau.

Lost property

Schnitzlergasse 6, opposite the Town Hall. Tel. 32240.

Oberammergau Museum

Showing Bavarian art, crafts and culture, Dorfstraße 8. Open
10 a.m. – 5 p.m. December–January and April–October, from
Tue.–Sun. and holidays. Tel. 94136. In non-Play years you can
buy a single ticket to include both the Museum and a tour of
the Theatre. E-mail: museum@oberammergau.de

Passion Play Theatre

Tel. 9458833 for opening hours and guided tours in non-Play
years, when there is an English tour April–October daily at 11
a.m. and 2 p.m. E-mail: passionstheater@oberammergau.de

Pilatushaus

See woodcarvers and other craftsmen at work, Ludwig-
Thoma-Str. 10. Admission free, mid-May–October Tue.–Sat.
1 p.m. – 6 p.m. Tel. 949511. E-mail: info@oberammergau.de

Post office

Deutsche Bundespost, Rottenbucherstraße 36. Tel. 3061.
Open 8.30 a.m. – 5 p.m. Monday to Friday and until noon
on Saturday.

Railway station

Bahnhofstraße. Tel. 3513.

Souvenirs

Oberammergau is famous for its woodcarvings, and you can
buy delightful toys, Christmas cribs and decorations, and
clocks, but they are not cheap, so allow enough currency or
credit cards to bring back what you want. There are also items
of embroidery, *dirndl* dresses, Tyrolean hats and other items
of outdoor clothing, and of course books, postcards, transparencies and CDs of the Passion Play; DVDs and videos of the

region but not of the Play. (UK visitors should be sure to buy the British PAL version of videos and the European region 2 of DVDs, though videos are rapidly being replaced by DVDs.)

Taxis

Richter, Welfengasse 2. Tel. 94294.
Götz, Schmädlgasse 12. Tel. 94440.

Weather forecasts

You can find weather forecasts for Oberammergau on http://weather.yahoo.com/forecast/GMXX2959.html or in German on wetter.com

WellenBerg Leisure Centre

Swimming pools, sauna, solarium, hot-air balloon, etc. Himmelreich 52, open daily, May–September 9.30 a.m. – 9 p.m.; October–April 10 a.m. – 9 p.m. Telephone 92360. E-mail: wellenberg@oberammergau.de

Location of Oberammergau in Europe

Part 1
Visiting Oberammergau

History

The Oberammergau Passion Play is unique because it has been performed regularly without interruption for over 350 years, and because it originated with a vow made to God in 1633 at the time of an outbreak of the plague.

The bubonic plague is a disease transmitted by fleas, which infect people they bite with the bacillus *Yersinia pestis*. An early symptom is a painful swelling of lymph nodes, usually in the armpit and groin; such swellings are called 'buboes'. It causes virulent blood poisoning and the death rate is high. In the children's rhyme, the 'ring of roses' is the rash by which the plague was recognized, the 'pocketful of posies' was the bunch of flowers people carried to ward off the smell of death and corruption, and after a sneezing fit most of the sufferers did indeed fall down – dead. In many cities the wagons went round with the cry 'Bring out your dead', of which there were so many that they were often dumped in a mass grave or plague pit. Between a third and a half of the population of Europe died of the Black Death in the fourteenth century.

The Thirty Years' War in the early seventeenth century was between different princes all over Europe attempting to settle whether the areas they dominated should follow Roman Catholic or Protestant versions of Christianity. The sense of community was so strong that both sides regarded it as essential that all the Christians in each town should worship at the same church, and eventually it was settled that different areas should follow different practices: 'to each region its own religion'. At the end of the war many out-of-work soldiers were tramping back home across Europe and, with the breakdown of law and order and of basic hygienic practices, they were accompanied by large numbers of black rats, each of which bore plague-infected fleas.

The villagers of Oberammergau hoped to keep themselves free of the plague, which was decimating surrounding communities, by isolating themselves. They set watchmen on the roads, who lit bonfires so that even at night they could see anyone approaching the Village and keep them out, in case they were carrying the plague.

But one man, who had left Oberammergau to seek work elsewhere, wanted to return to see the bride he had recently married, and he knew a way to slip past the watchmen. The present this home-comer brought with him to his native Village was the bubonic plague, and the burial registers show that in the next few months, out of a population of only about 600, 84 died from it.

The Vow

The Village elders met in the Parish Church to pray about this crisis. The church has since been rebuilt, but the crucifix before which they prayed still hangs to the right of the sanctuary in the present church. They made a vow, promising that, if the plague stopped in their Village, they would perform a Passion Play every ten years.

Nobody can force God to make a bargain with them: he is too great to need anything we can offer him. We shall never know whether that is what the Oberammergau elders thought they were doing, or whether it was a sincere promise of a gesture of thanksgiving if God condescended to have pity on them. Neither can we know why God sometimes gives to some people exactly what they pray for, and to others he says 'No,' or 'Wait,' or 'I have something better to give you instead, though you may not recognize it yet as such.' Jesus himself, in the Garden of Gethsemane, prayed to be spared from drinking the cup of suffering, yet he had to drink it to the dregs.

The prayer of the elders, however, was answered to the letter. From that day nobody else died of the plague in

Oberammergau. The next year, 1634, the first Oberammergau Passion Play was performed in a meadow in front of the church. From 1680 they decided to hold it at the beginning of each decade, and, with the exception of 1770 when it was forbidden and 1940 during the Second World War, it has been produced every ten years ever since. The missing dates were compensated for by extra performances on the 300th and 350th anniversaries of the first performance, in 1934 and 1984. Still today, the people of the Village meet in the Theatre a year before the Passion Play season and solemnly renew their vow.

Motives

Why, then, do the people of Oberammergau continue to produce the Play every ten years? Is it to fulfil an ancient vow, or just to become rich?

It is commonly said that none of the actors at Oberammergau is paid. That is not strictly true, for they are all compensated for loss of earnings, and nowadays those taking the principal characters, who have to give up their regular employment for the season, are paid a small salary. One of the actors performing Jesus calculated that he was paid €1 per hour. So nobody becomes rich by taking part in the Play.

The Golden Calf

Providing food and accommodation for guests, and making and selling souvenirs, are hard work and time consuming, and nobody would do it unless they expected to make some profit out of it. These things are lucrative in Passion Play years, and some of that income spreads to other villagers also by way of trade. In the nine years between Passion Plays, however, although Oberammergau works hard to attract tourists to come for other reasons, many restaurants and guest houses have to close, and some people live off their savings.

The profit on the Passion Play, from the difference between the sale of tickets and the costs of the production, is always spent on municipal projects of benefit to residents and visitors alike. A superb complex of swimming pools, with an exciting wave machine, has been developed. Cable cars have been taken up the mountains. The 'Ammergauer Haus' is a comfortable hall which serves as an administrative centre, for community meetings, and hosts exhibitions. A retractable roof is planned to cover the stage of the Passion Theatre, so that it can be used for operas and other shows during non-Play years. All these are paid for from the profits on the Play.

In spite of the great sacrifices the villagers make, of time, convenience and effort, they come in for criticism for being too commercially minded. It would be more charitable to think of the service they perform in enabling 4,700 visitors at a time, five times a week, to share in their act of worship, by bringing before us, in a way that we may never before have understood, the great love of Jesus in sacrificing his life that we might be forgiven. How anyone can complain of discomfort, criticize or hate others, after seeing that, defies comprehension.

Still a Village

Although it is unlike anywhere else on earth, Oberammergau is still a village. The hay is still brought in to feed the cows through the winter, at all available hours throughout the Play season. The cowsheds stand in the middle of the town, smelling just the same as every other cowshed, and much like the stable where the baby Jesus was born.

No wigs or false beards are used, so from Ash Wednesday in

the previous year everyone with a part in the Play, apart from the Roman soldiers, has to grow his or her hair to the appropriate length. Thus you will find the postman cycling round with a full patriarchal beard and flowing locks, and among the younger children it is hard to tell the boys from the girls. There is something very moving in seeing 'Jesus' riding past on a green bicycle, or in being served in his shop by 'St Peter'. It helps us to a deeper understanding of Jesus, reminding us that he was apparently just like all the villagers of his time. 'Is not this the carpenter's son?' asked the people of Nazareth. 'He had no form or comeliness that we should admire him,' prophesied Isaiah. It was only as his disciples came to know him closely, and saw the great love in his heart for everyone, including the outcast and despised, that they realized he might be more than merely human. For they recognized that the love he showed was like the compassion he described in God his heavenly Father. Many people today admire Jesus as a man and a prophet, but not until they have known him for a long time as a friend are they ready to acknowledge him by any grander title. Surely he accepts that?

One time I went to hire a bicycle from one of the carpenters of Oberammergau at his workshop. As he adjusted the saddle height for me, I noticed that his brawny hands were stained red. Alarmed that he had cut himself, I asked if that was his blood on his hands. 'No,' he replied, with a wry smile. 'That is the blood of Christ – I'm the soldier who nails him to the cross!' I knew, and he knew that I knew, that it was only paint. But what effect is it going to have on a man to know that, even if only symbolically, he has the blood of Christ on his hands five times a week for five months?

The villagers of Oberammergau, they would be the first to admit, are not all perfect. Most of them are a mixture of quiet saint and noisy sinner like the rest of us. Living with the re-enactment of the death of Jesus as the centre of Village life, however, seems to have an effect, and each of them is probably just a little better than they would have been if they lived somewhere else. It shows, in the courtesy and kindness with which they treat the crowds of visitors who disrupt the life of their Village when they come to see the Play.

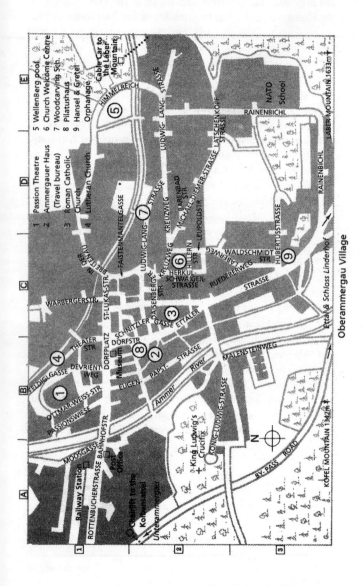

1 Passion Theatre
2 Ammergauer Haus (Travel bureau)
3 Roman Catholic Church
4 Lutheran Church
5 Wellenberg pool
6 Church Welcome Centre
7 Woodcarving Sch.
8 Hansel & Gretel
9 Orphanage

Oberammergau Village

6

Streetlist for the Oberammergau Village Plan opposite

(*A larger plan of the village and its outskirts is available from the* Oberammergau Tourist Information Office, Ammergauer Haus, Eugen-Papst-Straße 9a, D-82487 Oberammergau, Germany. *Open Monday to Friday 9 am to 6 pm, Saturday 9 am to 12 noon.* Telephone +49 (0) 8822 9231-0, Fax 9231-90 info@oberammergau.de)

Bahnhofstraße A-1
Bärenbadstraße D-2
Daisenbergerstraße C-2
Devrientweg B-1
Dorfplatz B-1 (*this is now named Dorfstraße, and is pedestrianised with a diversion around the Theatre for vehicles*)
Dorfstraße B-1
Eugen-Papst-Straße B-1
Ettaler Straße C-2
Faistenmantelgasse C-1
Feldiglgasse B-1
Herkul.-Schwaiger-Straße C-2
Hillernstraße C-2
Himmelreich E-1
Hubertusstraße C-3
In der Breitenau C-1

König-Ludwig-Straße B-2
Laberweg C-3
Latschenkopfstraße D-2
Kreuzweg C-2
Leupoldstraße C-2
Ludwig-Lang-Straße C-2
Malensteinweg B-3
Michael-Diemer-Straße D-2
Moosgasse A-1
Ottmar-Weiß-Straße B-1
Passionswiese B-1
Rainenbichl D-3
Rottenbucherstraße A-1
Ruedererweg C-3
Schnitzlergasse C-2
St.-Lukas-Straße C-1
Theaterstraße B-1
Waldschmidtstraße C-3
Warbergerstraße C-1

Features of Interest

Oberammergau is an excellent centre for walking or cycling in summer and skiing in winter. A cable car carries visitors up the Laber Mountain to walk from the top. The chair lift almost opposite the railway station takes one to the ridge, along which a walk and a scramble lead to the cross on the top of the Koffel, the sugar-loaf shaped mountain that dominates Oberammergau.

The walls of the houses, like many in the region, are decorated with paintings. Many are scenes from the Bible or the lives of the saints, and paintings of the crucifixion remind us that, in many ways, Oberammergau is a village under the cross. These wall-paintings are referred to locally as *Lüftlmalerei* – paintings in the air. The paint is applied while the plaster is still wet. The Village orphanage is covered with scenes from the story of Hansel and Gretel.

There is a good museum of local crafts near the centre of the main street. Then, in the Pilatushaus, behind the Ammergauer Haus, there is often a local craftsman at work. The Pilatushaus is covered in staircases and balconies which are not real, but painted on the walls in *trompe l'oeil* (deceiving the eye) style; it is named after a wall-painting of Jesus on trial before Pontius Pilate. See above, pages xviii–xxii for opening times and telephone numbers.

The villagers have for centuries made a living selling wood-carvings. Hawkers from Oberammergau used to leave the Village with frames on their backs covered in carvings, and travel as far as the Baltic and Mediterranean seas, not returning until all their wares were sold many months later. Nowadays there is a school of woodcarving in Oberammergau. Even in their first few years at school, the children of the Village are watched to see whether they have talents in art, music or drama, and are then groomed from an early age to take a part in the Play, the choir or the orchestra, or to train as a woodcarver.

In the years when the Play is not being performed, visitors are taken backstage in the Passion Theatre, to see the machinery for the scenery of the tableaux, and many rooms full of costumes.

1 Oberammergau, King Ludwig's Crucifixion Group

2 Wall-painting of the taking of the vow

3 Oberammergau Lutheran Church

4 The leap of faith: Paraglider launching from the Laber mountain

5 Oberammergau Village from the Crucifixion Group

6 Woodcarving of the crucifixion and the Last Supper in the Parish Church

7 Oberammergau Parish Church

8 Inside the Parish Church at Mass

9 The crucifix in the Parish Church, before which the Vow was made

10 Palm Sunday procession figure in the Parish Church

11 The Pilatus House

12 Front of the Passion Play Theatre

13 Costumes for the Roman Soldiers

14 Leonhard Höldrich jun., woodcarver

Oberammergau is very ecologically conscious, and neither litter nor pollution is tolerated.

King Ludwig's Cross

King Ludwig II (see under Linderhof below, page 15) was a great patron of the arts, and he arranged for a private performance of the Oberammergau Passion Play, after which he gave each of the leading actors a silver spoon. Many of the Passion Plays at that time were very crude, with scenes such as whooping demons prancing around the dead Judas Iscariot, whose bowels gushing out were realistically represented with black sausages. So the Passion Plays were suppressed throughout the area as a harmful influence, with the exception of Oberammergau, where it was saved by the personal intervention of the King.

Ludwig II erected a statue of Christ on the cross, with the Virgin Mary and the Apostle John, on a hillside above the Village, as his personal tribute to the Passion Play. At the time it was erected it was the largest stone monument in Europe.

Accommodation

At one time, many visitors to the Passion Play stayed in a European resort hotel and were bussed into the Village and out again on the same day. This was a shame, as they only had a limited opportunity to meet the villagers and visit the local sites and shops. To counter this, most Play tickets are now sold as part of an 'arrangement', with accommodation in the Oberammergau region included. Because of the pressure on space, nobody can stay in the Village during the Passion Play for more than two nights, and only for one if they are seeing the Play on a Friday, though Saturday's performances are intended for those who are not staying in the Village. Some stay in hotels and guest houses; others are accommodated in the homes of villagers, and they can be heard joyfully exchanging the information that they have been staying with the High Priest Caiaphas or Joseph of Arimathea, since most households in the Village have at least one family member with a part in the Play.

Transport from where visitors are staying to and from the Theatre is included in the price of the tickets.

Many of the villagers, then, have to work in three ways during the Play season:

- they continue to do the work that employs them during the other nine years;
- they are involved in the Play – 1,000 villagers, including children, out of a population of about 5,000, are on stage at some point, with 150 speaking roles, and 19 main characters each of which is played by two actors alternately. Another 400 are involved either behind the scenes or in the choir or orchestra;
- third, in their own homes or helping in the hotels, guest houses and restaurants, they have to feed nearly 5,000 visitors for each performance, change the sheets and clean their rooms after they have left.

Acting is emotionally draining. So is being nice to people they have never seen before, who do not speak the same language, and who may be irritable after a tiring journey. It is small wonder that the entire population of Oberammergau is exhausted by the end of the season. For them, producing the Passion Play every ten years is a real sacrifice. It would be easier if they catered for half as many visitors every five years. 'But', they reply, 'that was not what we vowed.'

Growing Numbers of Visitors

For the first 200 years the villagers of Oberammergau performed the Passion Play for their own benefit, in fulfilment of the vow, and to the glory of God. Then the railway was built as far as Weilheim, from where a coach and horses could be hired to drag travellers up the muddy and often dangerous tracks to the top of the Ammer Valley. The road was not metalled until 1889, but the railway was extended to Murnau in 1880, and then to Garmisch Partenkirchen by 1890. Now most visitors come by road in diesel coaches on 'arrival and departure' days.

In 1871 the future King Edward VII of England and his wife visited the Oberammergau Passion Play, vainly attempting to do so incognito. With this example, a visit to Oberammergau became fashionable and, already in 1910, almost 5,000 people at a time were coming in and out for a total of fifty-six performances. Still today nearly 40 per cent of the visitors are from countries of the English-speaking world.

Package or Pilgrimage?

Travellers have been described as those who don't know where they are going, and tourists as those who don't know where they have been. In that case pilgrims are those who set out for a place where they can meet God, and find that God has been with them throughout the journey.

Sadly, some of the visitors come as part of a package tour of Europe, and without suitable preparation they are baffled by the long and stately performance, when their normal experience of drama has been half-hour 'soaps' on television. Also, not everybody is well informed about the life of Jesus.

This book aims to turn a package tour into a pilgrimage. Whatever hardships the pilgrims of the Middle Ages had to bear, and however much it cost them, they travelled with the expectation of receiving some spiritual benefit, and most of them did. While sitting and waiting for a Passion Play to begin, if not before, it is good to pray for all who take part, all the spectators, and for yourself, that all may come away with a deeper love for God and a stronger desire to love and serve our neighbours.

Nearby Places of Interest

Ettal and Unterammergau

Because of the shortage of accommodation in Oberammergau, many visitors to the Passion Play stay in hotels and guest houses in Ettal, about seven kilometres (four miles) up the Ammer River; or Unterammergau, which is about the same distance downstream the other side of Oberammergau; or in the other villages. From these locations they are taken to the Play on regular shuttle buses.

The priests of Oberammergau at the time of the vow were supplied from the monastery at Ettal. It was one of them, Father Othmar Weis, who wrote the earliest surviving text of the Oberammergau Passion Play. This text was revised in 1860 by Pastor Alois Daisenberger, whose version is the basis of the one used today.

Ettal monastery was founded in 1330 by Ludwig the Bavarian, an Emperor of the Holy Roman Empire, as a thanksgiving when he first set foot in Germany on returning from fierce battles near Rome. The original foundation was for twenty Benedictine monks and thirteen knights with their families. Ludwig brought with him from Italy a statue of the Virgin Mary in white Carrara marble, carved by Tino di Camaino, which, in its niche behind the high altar, is still the focus of Ettal Abbey Church.

The church is round, in imitation of the Basilica of the Holy Sepulchre in Jerusalem. It was burnt down in 1744, and rebuilt in Rococo style. Whereas Baroque architecture is flamboyantly ornamented with rather static figures symmetrically arranged on either side, Rococo is not symmetrical and the figures and statues are full of restless movement. Josef Schmuzer was the architect at Ettal, and the 52 metre (170 feet) high dome was painted by Johann Jakob Zeiller from Reutte. It shows the Holy Trinity of God the Father, Jesus his Son, and the Holy Spirit represented by a dove, praised by the disciples of St Benedict, the monks and nuns who follow the Rule of St Benedict in the Benedictine order and the other orders that have grown out of it.

The Ettal monastery was closed in 1803, but was given back to the Benedictines in 1900. The community now run a school, maintain a life of prayer and worship, brew beer and distil liqueurs. A shop by the gateway to the monastery sells Christian books and souvenirs.

Unterammergau has an interesting church, built in 1709.

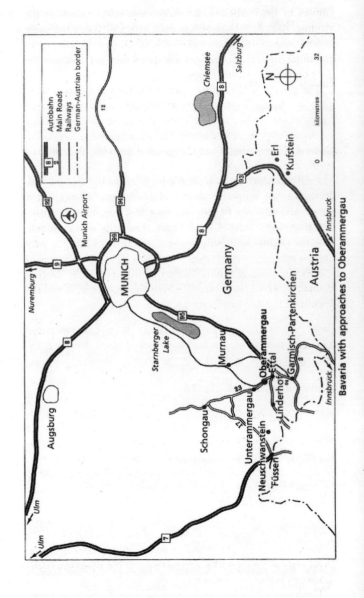

Bavaria with approaches to Oberammergau

Painted on the organ gallery is a stylized scene from the court of the Holy Roman Empire, which Voltaire described as neither holy, nor Roman, nor an empire.

Facilities in Ettal

Ettal has the same telephone dialling code as Oberammergau, 08822.

General information: www.kloster-ettal.de/index-uk.html

The Abbey: Open daily from 8 a.m. till 6 p.m. in winter and until 7.45 p.m. in summer, admission free. Times of service are shown at www.kloster-ettal.de/pfarrei/index.htm but this does not always correspond to the sign beside the abbey church door, so enquire locally.

Accommodation information: *Rathaus*, Ammergauer-Straße, D-82488 Ettal. Tel. 3534, Mon.–Fri. 8 a.m. – 12 noon, info@ettal.de

Cash: There is no bank, but there is a cash machine (*Geldautomat*) inside the building marked *Sparkasse*; enter by putting your card in the slot by the door.

Mountain rescue: Tel. 922688.

Police station: The nearest is in Oberammergau. Tel. 945830.

Facilities in Unterammergau

Unterammergau has the same telephone dialling code as Oberammergau, 08822.

Tourist-Information: Ammergauer Alpen GmbH, Rottenbucherstraße 9a. Tel. 922740.

Banks: *Kreissparkasse*, Dorfstraße. Tel. 94582, open Mon.–Wed. and Fri. 8 a.m. to 12 noon; Thu. 2 – 5.30 p.m.

V-R Raiffeisenbank, Dorfstraße. Tel. 4224, open Mon. and Fri. 8 a.m. to 12 noon, 2 – 4 p.m.; Tue.–Thu. 8 a.m. to 12 noon only; cash machine inside.

Police Station: The nearest is in Oberammergau, Tel. 945830.

Linderhof

About 10 kilometres or 6 miles from Oberammergau is the Castle of Linderhof, built by King Ludwig II. He became King of Bavaria in 1864 at the age of eighteen, following the death of his father Maximilian II. In contrast to his father's democratic style of rule, however, he aimed to be an absolute monarch after the style of Louis XIV of France, the 'Sun King', whose statue stands in the entrance hall at Linderhof. He was inspired by the Petit Trianon in Versailles to build a retreat at Linderhof where he could recreate the world of Wagner's *Tannhäuser*.

Visitors to Linderhof pass through the entrance hall and ascend the staircase to the Western Tapestry Room, where the walls are, in fact, decorated with paintings made to look like tapestries. Then the so-called 'Yellow Cabinet' is a room in the style of Louis XV of France, with Meissen porcelain wall-light fittings. The Audience Chamber has the King's throne behind a marble-topped desk, and the Lilac Cabinet beyond it also has fine Meissen porcelain. The Bedchamber is modelled on the Versailles custom of the monarch receiving his court as he rose in the morning and when he went to bed, though in fact the shy Ludwig II lived a solitary life. The view from the window is of the water cascade in the grounds, and among all the sumptuous decoration don't miss the Meissen porcelain either side of the window. The Pink Cabinet contains a portrait of Madame du Barry, the mistress of Louis XV; and there is more Meissen in the Dining Room, with a marble reproduction of the Venus of Medici. Then follow the Blue Cabinet and the Eastern Tapestry Room, which has a Sèvres porcelain peacock and a marble statue of the 'Three Graces'. Finally visitors pass through the Mirror Room, which must have looked incredible when lit by candles.

The grounds of Linderhof are beautifully laid out, with a fountain covered in gold leaf which normally plays every hour and rises high above the palace. The newly reconstructed Hundingshütte represents the first act of Wagner's *Walküre*. The Moorish Kiosk was bought by the King after the 1867 Paris Exhibition ended, and recreated in the grounds. The Venus Grotto reproduces the first act of Wagner's *Tannhäuser*. There the King could sit in a gilded shell-shaped boat on a lake surrounded by artificial stalactites and stalagmites, next to the crystal-covered 'Lorelei Cliff', and dream that he was in the world of romantic fables. Special operatic performances were mounted in the grotto for the King.

Ludwig II was engaged in January 1867 to Princess Sophie, the daughter of Duke Maximilian of Bavaria, but the engagement was broken off in October the same year. The essential loneliness of his life is shown by the table in the Linderhof dining room, which can be raised through the floor from the kitchen below, already laden with food, so that the King did not have to see any of his servants when he dined alone. He was deposed in 1886 because it was alleged that he was mad, and three days later was found drowned along with his psychiatrist in a few feet of water in the Starnberger Lake.

Linderhof is on an unnumbered road signposted 'Graswang' turning off the road from Oberammergau to Ettal. There are buses to Linderhof from Oberammergau railway station; book your bus ticket in advance from the Tourist Office, Ammergauer House, Eugen-Papst-Straße 9a, Oberammergau.

Facilities in Linderhof

The telephone dialling code in Linderhof is 08822, the same as Oberammergau, Ettal and Unterammergau.

Information office: *Staatliche Verwaltung*, D-82488 Ettal-Linderhof. Tel. 920349. Open daily April–September 9 a.m. to 6 p.m.; October–March 10 a.m. to 4 p.m. Admission charge; guided tours max. 40 people, write in for specific times or special tours; coach park. Internet: www.linderhof.de

Part 2
The Passion Play

Mystery Plays

The Oberammergau Passion Play is an example of the mystery plays of the Middle Ages. This is a form of drama of which few people today have much experience, but to appreciate fully what happens in Oberammergau we need to know something of the background.

Although the Christian Church resisted the classical theatre of Greece and Rome because of its association with immorality, the origins of modern drama are to be found in the church liturgy. The Holy Communion, Eucharist or Mass is a regular re-enactment or re-presentation, as Jesus commanded us, of the Last Supper which he held with his disciples. At Easter, in particular, the priests in the medieval Church made a symbolic visit to a part of the church representing the tomb where Jesus had been buried, acting out the early morning search of the women disciples for the body of the Christ.

In a period when few people could read the Scriptures, liturgical drama, along with stone carving and stained-glass windows, became the 'poor man's Bible'. In many places, the dramas grew into spectacles, lasting all day, portraying the whole life of Christ, and performed on carts and temporary stages at various places around the town. Each scene was allocated to an appropriate trade guild, so that, for instance, the schoolmasters might re-enact Jesus at the age of 12 disputing with the teachers of the law in the Temple, and the carpenters were responsible for the crucifixion scene.

These were called 'mystery plays', from St Paul's use of the word 'mystery' to mean God's secret plan to save us from sin and death by the life and death of Jesus, now revealed and

Cleansing the Temple

made public to everyone. The texts of the medieval cycles of plays are preserved in York, Coventry and some other places in England, where in recent years they have been regularly performed. The well-known 'Coventry Carol' comes from the Coventry Mystery Plays, and is the lullaby sung by the mothers of Bethlehem to their babies who were about to be slaughtered by King Herod's soldiers.

Unlike these representations of the whole of Christ's life, those of the Alpine region concentrated on the events of his last week. They are called 'passion plays' from the Latin word *passus* meaning 'suffered'. We use the word in the same way in the name of the passion flower, parts of which resemble the nails, whips, and crown of thorns from the story of the crucifixion of Jesus. Unlike the mystery plays, the passion plays were performed on a fixed, if temporary, stage. The people of the Middle Ages wanted a good number of demons in their passion plays, so they usually concluded with a scene of the Last Judgement. These seem crude to modern tastes, so have usually been excised from the texts that are performed today.

Choosing the Actors

Anyone who wishes to act, sing or play in the Passion Play must have been born in Oberammergau or have lived there for at least 20 years. The major parts are now each performed by two actors taking turns in alternate performances. They are all elected by a committee, who announce their decision to great excitement a year before the first performance. From May 2009, details can be obtained from tour operators, or from http://www.oberammergau.de

Previously any woman appearing on stage had to be unmarried, but since 1990 the part of the Virgin Mary has sometimes been taken by a married woman with children.

Part way through the 2000 season, one of the married women who had been singing in the chorus had a baby in the local hospital. For one of the last performances, she carried him on to the stage during the Triumphal Entry scene, claiming that he had the right to appear in the Play as he had been born in the village. The actor performing the part of Jesus got down from his donkey to pat the baby on the head, saying he had never before seen anyone so young on the stage. But the child's father had not lived in the village long enough, so was not allowed to take part.

PRACTICAL DETAILS

In this section we will cover the things that every pilgrim needs to know when they attend the Passion Play. (See also 'Practical Information', page xviii above.)

In 2010 the Play will be performed five times a week, from 2.30 p.m. to about 5 p.m.; then, after a three hour break, the second part will last from 8 until 10.30 p.m.

Tickets

The seats are all numbered, and each ticket shows the door through which to enter. From all seats there is a good view of the stage, and the acoustics in the Passion Theatre are excellent. There are four categories of ticket depending on the type of accommodation you are staying at in the Village.

The price of the one-night package (Friday performances only except 1 October) includes one overnight stay including breakfast; hot lunch or lavish brunch before the play starts; hot dinner with several courses during the play interval; shuttle service in Oberammergau and the nearby villages; local assistance; admission ticket to the Passion Play in the respective category; programme book of the 2010 Passion Play; admission ticket for the Oberammergau Museum, and local tax. For the two-night package (Sunday, Tuesday and Thursday performances except 3 October) it is the same, except that there are two overnight stays including breakfast, and hot dinner on the day of arrival.

Tickets without accommodation, intended for those who can reach Oberammergau conveniently in a day's journey, for Saturday performances only (plus 1 and 3 October but not 2 October), will be sold from spring 2009 direct from:

Office of the Passion Play 2010,
Oberammergau and DER Reiseburo oHG,
Eugen-Papst-Str. 9a, 82487 Oberammergau, Germany.
Tel. +49 (0) 8822 92 31-0, Fax 92 31-52.
Internet: www.passionspiele2010.de
E-mail: info@passionspiele2010.de

They are mostly sold out months, even years, in advance.

Clothing

The audience is under cover but the stage is not. Some people say that the weather changes four times each day in Oberammergau. So it is advisable to wear layers of clothing that can be put on or taken off as it becomes colder or warmer. It can be very cold, so the Theatre and the shops nearby also hire blankets to wrap round you if required. In case it rains on the way to the Theatre, taking a pair of slippers would avoid having to sit in wet shoes.

Seating

The seats are fairly comfortable, with under-floor heating. Even so, it is wise to bring, or to hire from the shops near the Theatre, a pillow or cushion to ease sitting still for five and a half hours.

Toilets

There are toilets near the entrance doors, accessible from the outside (though you may re-enter on showing your ticket), and near the stage, accessible from inside the Theatre.

Open-air stage

The stage is in the open air. This does not mean that you can sneak a view of the action if you have no ticket: there are walls at the sides. The backdrop is formed by a ridge of mountains, with constantly changing patterns of sun and clouds. Sometimes it happens that there is a dramatic thunderstorm at the time of the crucifixion.

Rain

The audience is under cover, but the retractable roof over the stage which is planned for operas in non-Play years will not be used for the Passion Play. The cast will get wet if it rains; but there are a row of hair-driers and a change of costumes backstage if this happens, and the choir can wear raincoats under their robes. Plastic sheets protect the front few rows of the audience. The orchestra, which is in a pit below the front of the stage, is moved under cover, because it is impossible to play a wet violin. In 2000, the season was extended by a few weeks, and near the end it snowed on stage. The actor playing Jesus said the hardest thing he had to do was to stop shivering when he was supposed to be dead.

English translation

Most visitors, unless they have fluent German, will need to have an English translation of the Play. These are on sale in many hotels, in shops that display the sign *Textbuch*, and inside and outside the Theatre. While nobody would want to miss any of the action while their head is buried in a book, there is usually time during the sung choruses to read what is going to happen next. Even those who are entirely familiar with the events of the Gospels may need the text to see what connections are being made with the Old Testament scenes.

Meals

Tour operators or those who provide accommodation may provide meal tickets for selected restaurants serving only environmentally friendly food. There are many good restaurants, or you may buy sandwiches to eat in the open air.

Cameras

The villagers see the Passion Play as an act of worship. Therefore they want no applause, and cameras and camcorders are not allowed in the Theatre. Not only is it totally ineffective to use a flash-camera in a building of that size, it is grossly discourteous to one's neighbours, who may be praying or in tears, to give the Play the atmosphere of a spectacle or a press conference. Excellent transparencies of the current year's Play can be purchased, or postcards, or a picture book, to show friends at home; they are far better than an amateur photographer could take. There are also CDs of the music.

If you should find yourself sitting next to somebody who insists on using a camera during the Passion Play, or talking, or rustling sweet papers, it will not help you or anybody else to gain more spiritual benefit from the Play by getting angry. The best advice is silently to pray for your neighbour.

DVDs

There are DVDs promoting tourism to the Village, but at present none of the Play itself. The villagers, rightly or wrongly, reply that they do not want their act of worship reproduced in people's living rooms.

THE TEXT OF THE PASSION PLAY

Changes in the Text

The villagers of Oberammergau voted to continue using the text of the Passion Play that was written in 1870 by Joseph Alois Daisenberger, replacing an even older text. But each time the Play is performed, small changes are introduced to that text, and lines or scenes missed out, to bring it more in tune with modern thinking. The style of the production tries to reflect the way modern Christians speak about Jesus.

The Director of the production in 1990, 2000 and again in 2010 is Christian Stückl, a man from Oberammergau who has become a famous theatre director in Munich. The Second Director is Otto Huber, who feels passionately about the text of the Passion, and together they have produced a revision. They have been advised by Ludwig Mödl, professor of Pastoral Theology at the University of Munich, and adviser to both the Roman Catholic and the Lutheran bishops' conferences.

They have made Jesus an even stronger figure than before, and have also brought out the strength of personality in the Virgin Mary and Mary Magdalene. Some new *tableaux-vivants* have been added, showing Moses as a saviour of his people, foreshadowing Jesus. They have brought back, with new words, some of the music of Rochus Dedler, which had been omitted when more obscure scenes were dropped in previous years. Completely new costumes and scenery were introduced in 2000.

Jesus prays in the Temple

Anti-Semitism

Although few Germans alive in 2010 were old enough at the time of the holocaust to influence events, they are very conscious that false interpretations of some passages in the Gospels, down the years, have led to prejudice against Jewish people. Such passages have been left out of successive revisions of the text in Oberammergau, and the scenery and costumes emphasize that Jesus and his followers all belonged to the Jewish race. Judas Iscariot is no longer shown as mad or evil but as a human being who made disastrously wrong choices. Jesus' teaching in the Sermon on the Mount, although it occurred earlier in Galilee, is likely to have been repeated by him on numerous occasions, and is shown as the reason for his condemnation. Subtle changes are also made in the presentation of Pontius Pilate, King Herod and the Jewish leaders.

In particular, those Jewish leaders who opposed the crucifixion have been made prominent, to show that the disputes that led up to that terrible event were disputes within

Judaism over the interpretation of the Jewish Scriptures, not between Christians and Jews.

Three, or maybe all four, of the Gospels were written by Jews. When St John's Gospel speaks of 'the Jews' who opposed Jesus, he probably meant the High Priests and others in authority, not the common people. When St Matthew reported that the crowd cried 'His blood be on us and on our children' (Matthew 27.25, a phrase not included in the modern text of the Play), he was probably thinking of the redeeming effect of sacrificial blood, not of guilt. Many passages have been misinterpreted in the past to justify racial prejudice, but that was not their original purpose.

No excuse can be made for anti-Semitism in the past, but the villagers hope the Passion Play will discourage it in future. Whatever our race, they say, we are all guilty of the type of sin that caused the death of Jesus, and all equally blessed by his love.

A number of Jewish organizations protested in 2000 that the Oberammergau Passion Play still showed signs of German anti-Semitism. This distressed those who had worked so hard on the text. It is difficult to see what more could be done to promote racial harmony when depicting the crucifixion of Jesus the Jew.

THE SHAPE OF THE PLAY

The Play begins with verses spoken by the Prologue. Then the large choir sings a meditation on the events we are about to see, and how they are the fulfilment of the promises made in the Jewish Scriptures.

Next the choir divides and the curtains at the back of the stage open to reveal a *tableau-vivant* (living picture) of a scene from the Scriptures. These stationary scenes, which used to be quite common in theatrical performances, are seldom seen anywhere other than Oberammergau these days. It is a marvel how still the actors, including young children, can hold their pose for a minute or so until the curtains close again.

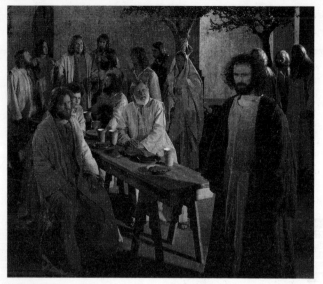

In Bethany

Typology

The tableaux rely on the system known as 'typology', which finds events in the Hebrew Scriptures that resemble events in the New Testament. The resemblances are often allegorical, and sometimes quite obscure, but at the time the Play was written this was the normal way of interpreting the Old Testament.

The Apocrypha

One of the tableaux is usually taken from the Book of Tobit. When St Paul wrote that 'all Scriptures are inspired by God' (2 Timothy 3.16) he was probably thinking of the Greek Bible, which includes Tobit and several other books not found in the Hebrew version. They are therefore included in the Old Testament section of Roman Catholic and Eastern Orthodox Bibles. Lutherans, Anglicans, and some other Protestants, however, call them the 'Apocrypha' (meaning 'hidden'), and insert them between the Old and New Testaments.

Palm Sunday

Then the choir leave the stage and a scene from the Gospels begins. The Play opens with the events of Palm Sunday. There is always a gasp of delight from the audience when the actor portraying Jesus enters, riding on a donkey which seems hardly big enough to carry him. During the season in 2000 the donkey gave birth to a foal, which came on stage with her, so that they could follow St Matthew's version, which says that Jesus was 'riding on an ass and a colt the foal of an ass'. The colt was naughty, though, and the disciples had to beware he didn't nip them. Around 600 people are on stage to wave palm branches and welcome Jesus to Jerusalem.

The Fickleness of Crowds

The crowd welcomed Jesus because they expected the Messiah to drive out the occupying Roman army, but they realized that this was not what he intended. So, later in the Play, the same crowd is easily whipped up by the leaders into shouting for the death of Jesus: 'Crucify him, crucify him!' The stage is so close to the audience that spectators feel almost as though they were part of that crowd. When we see how easily any crowd can be persuaded to do evil things by mass hysteria, we realize that we are all as much in need of the forgiveness that God offers as those who killed the Son of God.

Jesus in the Temple

When Jesus drives the traders from the Temple, it is impressive to see whole cages full of doves released and flying high into the sky above the Passion Theatre. But, of course, they will then fly off to a dovecote nearby, to be collected and returned to the Theatre for the next day's performance!

AN OUTLINE OF THE PLAY

This is the outline as it was performed in 2000. At the time of writing, it has not been decided what changes will be made in 2010. They will probably be minor, and some other *tableaux-vivants* may be substituted for those shown here. Reading this summary in advance will prepare you for what to expect, but you should follow the text book, on sale outside the Theatre, during the play, because it is an exact English translation of what is said on stage in German, or else the programme book issued with your ticket. If the words seem ponderous, remember that this was how Christians spoke in the nineteenth century.

FIRST SESSION

Prelude: Eternal life, which Adam lost at the tree of Paradise, is won back by Christ at the tree of the Cross.

Tableau-vivant: Adam is banished from Paradise *(Genesis 3)*, and the Cross is honoured.

Prologue. Chorus: 'God Eternal, hear your children.'

I Entry into Jerusalem

Jesus enters Jerusalem on a donkey. The crowd sings 'All praise, all praise, King David's Son' (see page 73). Jesus drives the traders from the Temple. The question about Jesus' authority. Reaction of the priests.

II The meal in Bethany, and Jesus' farewell to his Mother

Tableau-vivant: Tobias says farewell to his parents *(Tobit 5, Apocrypha)*, and leaves to bring salvation.

Tableau-vivant: The Bride in the Song of Solomon looks for her bridegroom *(Song of Songs 3, 6)*.

Jesus is received by his friends at Bethany, and anointed by Mary Magdalene. He predicts his suffering and death.

Jesus' concern for Judas. Jesus says farewell to his Mother Mary. Judas struggles with his doubts.

III Jesus denounces the Teachers of the Law – Preparation for the Arrest

Tableau-vivant: Moses, carrying the tablets with the commandments, finds the people worshipping a golden calf. *(Exodus 32)*

The Sermon on the Mount. Jesus denounces the Teachers of the Law and the Pharisees. The priests decide to imprison Jesus. Judas Iscariot offers to show them where he is to be found. For the life of Jesus, the purchase price of a slave is agreed on. The Supreme Council agrees on the death of Jesus, though some members disagree with the decision.

IV The Last Supper

Tableau-vivant: The Passover meal of the Israelites during the exodus from Egypt. *(Exodus 12)*

Jesus washes his disciples' feet and shares the meal of the Passover Lamb with them. His words of farewell.

V On the Mount of Olives

Tableau-vivant: General Amasa is treacherously stabbed to death by General Joab. *(1 Samuel 20)*

1 Judas leads the temple guard to Gethsemane.

Tableau-vivant: Moses meets God in a burning bush. *(Exodus 3)*

2 Jesus comforts his disciples and prays for them. Jesus prays in agony, and is strengthened by an angel. Judas betrays Jesus with a kiss. Jesus is arrested.

Chorus: 'Pain's grievous battle has begun.'

SECOND SESSION

VI Jesus is examined and mistreated by Annas – Peter denies that he knows Jesus, and his remorse

Tableau-vivant: Daniel is unjustly condemned to be thrown into a den of lions. *(Daniel 6)*

Tableau-vivant: Job is ridiculed because of his faith. *(Job 2)*
Annas the High Priest waits for Jesus, who is in prison. Judas learns that Jesus is going to die. Jesus is interrogated and struck. Peter, when ridiculed, denies knowing his Master.

VII Interrogation before Caiaphas
Judas's agony of conscience
Jesus is sentenced to death by the Supreme Council
Judas despairs

Tableau-vivant: Cain is conscience-stricken for killing his brother. *(Genesis 4)*
Judas suffers agonies of conscience. The Supreme Council disagree about whether Jesus is guilty. Jesus is led before Caiaphas, the other High Priest. Judas returns the 30 silver pieces, bewails his betrayal of Jesus, and hangs himself.

VIII Jesus before Pontius Pilate, and King Herod

Tableau-vivant: Moses before the Egyptian Pharaoh. *(Exodus 5)*
1. The leaders of the Council take Jesus before Pontius Pilate, the Roman Governor. The Priests accuse him of blasphemy, and of rebellion against the Roman Emperor, and demand the death penalty. Pilate interrogates Jesus and asks about his kingdom. Hearing that Jesus comes from Galilee, he refers him for trial by King Herod.
2. Herod asks Jesus to perform a miracle, dresses him as a king and mocks him. Herod sends Jesus back to Pilate.
3. The Priests bring Jesus again before Pilate. Pilate threatens to set Jesus free. Council members stir up the crowd to demand freedom for Barabbas instead of Jesus. Pilate's wife is frightened by a dream about Jesus. Pilate sends Jesus to

be whipped by the Roman soldiers. They put a purple robe around him and a crown of thorns on his head and pretend to honour him as a king.

Tenor solo and Choir: 'Behold the king . . . behold the man.'

IX   *Jesus is condemned to death on the cross*

Tableau-vivant: In contrast to Jesus, Joseph is acclaimed by the people as their Saviour. *(Genesis 41)*

The disciples are alarmed by the crowd, who call for Jesus to be crucified. Pilate recognizes that the mob is not representative of the people of Jerusalem. Nevertheless, Pilate releases Barabbas and condemns Jesus to death on the cross. He washes his hands to show he is not guilty.

X   *The Way of the Cross to the place of execution on the hill of Golgotha – the suffering and death of Jesus on the cross*

Tableau-vivant: Abraham is ready to offer his son Isaac as a sacrifice, and the son himself carries the wood for the sacrifice to Mount Moriah. *(Genesis 22)*

Tableau-vivant: Looking at the bronze snake, which Moses lifts up, brings healing and salvation when in danger of death. *(Numbers 21, John 3.14)*

1. Mary follows her son on the way of the cross. Carrying his cross, Jesus is led out to Golgotha. Mary meets her son. Simon of Cyrene helps Jesus to carry the cross. Jesus meets the women of Jerusalem. Veronica wipes his face with a cloth.

Prologue: 'Up, good people . . . '

2. Jesus is lifted up on the cross and mocked. The last words of Jesus and his death. The soldier's spear pierces Jesus' heart. Joseph of Arimathea requests permission to bury the body. The High Priests demand a guard to keep watch over it. Jesus is taken down from the cross and laid in his Mother's arms.

Song at the Tomb: 'All you who pass by, behold and see such love.'

XI *'On the third day he rose again in accordance with the Scriptures; he ascended into heaven and is seated at the right hand of the Father!'*

Prologue: Christ is risen from the tomb.

The angel shows the women the empty tomb. Christ appears to Mary Magdalene.

Final tableau: Hallelujah! Praise the one who conquers death!

AFTER SEEING THE PLAY

Historical accuracy

How historical is the Passion Play? Apart from the tradition about Veronica wiping the face of Jesus on his way to Golgotha, everything portrayed in the Play is taken from the Old Testament, the Apocrypha, or the Gospels of Matthew, Mark, Luke or John. Many scholars seem to be returning to the view that at least one and maybe all four Gospels could have been written before, or soon after, Jerusalem was destroyed by the Romans in AD 70, about 40 years after the resurrection of Jesus. Anyone who is more than 40 years old will agree that 40 years is a very short time! If anyone now tried to pass off as true an inaccurate account of what happened 40 years ago, there would be any number of eye-witnesses around to object. So, although some of the sayings from earlier in the life of Jesus have been transposed to Holy Week for dramatic effect in the Passion Play, and allowing for a tendency to make the Last Supper, for instance, look more like an Old Master painting than the reality actually was, we may say that what appears on the stage in Oberammergau is very nearly what happened in Jerusalem two thousand years ago. In fact some have said that attending the Passion Play is second only to a pilgrimage to the Holy Land as a way of meeting the real Jesus face to face.

Jesus washes the disciples' feet

Reactions

When they come out of the Passion Play Theatre, different people react in different ways to what they have seen. I met some who had wept at the story of the unjust death of a good man, but did not believe that Jesus was anything more than that. Jesus himself said, 'Weep not for me but for yourselves.'

Some react with puzzlement. When people say they have no faith, they often mean that the picture of God they have been given is not big enough to meet their problems. They need a larger idea of God.

In particular they need to see that God made human beings so that they should return his love, and for that to be possible he had to make it possible for us to reject him and hurt each other. But God's way of dealing with sinners who oppress

33

others is not to destroy them, or there would be no hope for any of us. Instead, God suffers with the oppressed and loves the oppressors, in order to show them what they are doing.

The Cross of Christ

When we see a stone, metal or wooden crucifix, it is easy to forget that in crucifixion the Romans had acquired from the Persians the most painful method of execution ever invented. To see an actor in a passion play hanging on a cross for about 20 minutes, even though we know he is supported by a harness underneath his loincloth, brings many people for the first time to an understanding of what it cost Jesus to hang like that for three hours. Crucifixion was used for slaves and rebels, and involved fixing the arms at such an angle that the victim could not breathe except by pushing himself up on the nail through his feet, in order to gasp a breath, and then slumping down again, suspended by the nails through the wrists. After a few hours of this in the hot sun most criminals were too exhausted to continue, and died of suffocation. To ensure that they were dead, their legs were broken so that they could not lift themselves up any more. Jesus, however, had already died of a broken heart, so the soldiers did not need to break his legs, fulfilling the prophecy, 'Not a bone of him shall be broken.'

Jesus wanted us to see that his own self-sacrificing love for us is a reflection of the way God loves us. Many people have looked at the cross of Christ and realized that God shares all our pain and grief; it is a sort of 'cross-section' of the pain in the heart of God.

'Don't Mention the War'

I met one elderly Englishman coming out of the Oberammergau Lutheran Church in tears, and spoke sympathetically to him. 'It was saying the Lord's Prayer that finished me,' he explained. 'You see, I fought the Germans during the war; then today I knelt between two Germans and heard myself saying, "Forgive us our trespasses, as we forgive those who trespass against us."'

Talking

Jesus taught his followers to talk to God as naturally as children talk to their parents. Many visitors want to pray when they have seen the Passion Play. Simply talking to God in your own words is best, but this book contains some suggestions for those who find that difficult (page 68).

A little girl was once told, 'Think before you speak.' She replied, 'How can I know what I think until I've heard what I say?' Talking to others helps us to sort out our own ideas. Ministers of all denominations often find people want to talk with them after the Play. Sharing reactions to the Play with others on the journey home can also be useful.

It would be selfish to keep to ourselves any new insights into Jesus and God that we have found on our journey. So visitors usually want to tell their friends and neighbours about the Play when they reach home.

Many people react to the Play with a deeper commitment to God, or even by putting God in charge of their lives for the first time. They have seen what Jesus has done for them. In gratitude, they want to promise to pray more, and to love God and their neighbour more deeply. Telling somebody else about this decision is a way of showing that there will be no going back.

God Understands

Many go to Oberammergau angry with God because of what they are suffering. In comparison with the suffering of Jesus, our own pain pales to insignificance. Jesus said, 'I and the Father are one' (John 10.30). That means that God suffers too, because of our sins. So God understands all our trouble and bears it for us. I first attended the Passion Play soon after my son was killed by a drunk driver. But I looked at the crucifixion, and realized that God understands what it is like when one's son dies.

Part 3
Worship

To prepare yourself to see the Play, and to give thanks afterwards, you may wish to worship God with other Christians. In previous years the Play has been performed in two halves on the morning and afternoon of the same day; in 2010 it will be in the afternoon and evening, from 2.30–5 p.m. and 8–10.30 p.m. The change has been made to enable the increasing number of Oberammergau folk who work outside the Village to act in the Play after they return from work. But it will make it harder for people in the audience to attend a church service after the Play, and the churches are having to rethink the times of services. A leaflet from the churches will probably be handed out in the Village listing service times. Depending on the time you arrive and leave the Village, it is worthwhile to find where the churches are and make time for worship.

OBERAMMERGAU PARISH CHURCH

The Roman Catholic Church

The onion-shaped dome of the Roman Catholic Parish Church rises over the Village. The church was built in 1749 on the site of the church where the vow had been made. It was decorated by local artists in a blend of Baroque and Rococo styles.

There is a daily Mass, sometimes in German, sometimes in English or partly in each language, and visiting priests are invited to concelebrate (see contact details below, page 40).

The high altar

The theme of the high altar is the Rosary: St Dominic receives the string of rosary beads from the Virgin Mary, while St Catherine of Siena receives the crown of thorns from Jesus Christ.

The sanctuary

The statues in the sanctuary from left to right are: St Joseph with the child Jesus; St Peter with the cross on which he was crucified upside down (see below), the keys of the kingdom and a cock whose crowing marked Peter's betrayal; St Paul with the sword of the Spirit; St Joachim – in tradition, the husband of St Anne, who was the mother of the Virgin Mary – with doves.

The paintings on the walls of the sanctuary are, on the left, Jesus teaching the Lord's Prayer, and on the right the angel announcing to Mary that she will bear a son. The medallions in the sanctuary are the symbols of the four Gospels: an angel for St Matthew; an eagle for St John; a lion for St Mark and an ox for St Luke (Ezekiel 1.10).

The side altars

The side altars nearest the sanctuary are: on the left, the altar of the Holy Trinity, with statues of St Martin and St Gregory, and a painting, at the top, of the beheading of St Barbara. On the right is the altar of the Holy Cross – the crucifix, from the previous Gothic church, is the one before which the Village elders made their vow in 1633. The statues on this altar represent Dismas the good thief, Mary, John and Mary Magdalene; the painting at the top is of the beheading of St Catherine of Alexandria.

Next to the altar of the Holy Cross is a pietà, Mary cradling the body of her dead son, which is also from the Gothic church.

The side altars in the middle are: on the left, the altar of St Anne, with a painting and an old statue of Anne, Mary and Jesus, and statues of St Sebastian with a bow and St Rochus, both of whom were invoked against the plague. On the right is the altar of St Anthony of Padua, a Franciscan, with statues of St Clare and St Francis of Assisi, John the Baptist and St John Nepamuk.

The pulpit has a relief of Jesus the Good Shepherd.

The dome

Around the dome is a fresco showing Saints Peter and Paul, to whom the church is dedicated, saying farewell as they come out of the city of Rome to be martyred. Peter was crucified upside down (because he said he was not worthy to die in the same way as his Master), and Paul was beheaded with a sword, because Roman citizens could not be crucified. In the centre of the dome is the Holy Trinity, Father, Son and Holy Spirit surrounded by figures from the Bible. The medallions under the fresco represent St Augustine of Hippo (burning heart); Ambrose (bee-hive); Gregory (musical notes) and Jerome (books).

Above the organ loft there is a painting of the altar of St Peter's Basilica in Rome; there are scenes from the Bible on the galleries with, in the centre under the organ, Moses lifting up the bronze serpent.

Among the carvings in the church, that of Christ sitting on a donkey is on a pole ready to be used to lead the procession on Palm Sunday.

Passion Play model

Under the tower at the back of the church is a beautiful carved and painted wooden model of scenes from the Passion. Drop a €1 coin in the slot, and it will be illuminated to the accompaniment of music from the Play.

Choir and orchestra

Those who attend Sunday morning Mass in the Parish Church will find it led by the choir and orchestra who also perform at the Passion Play. They are all amateurs, but the word 'amateur' comes from the Latin *amor*, meaning love, and they all have an excellent standard. Somebody remarked that Noah's

The Last Supper

ark was built by amateurs, but the *Titanic* by professionals!

The grave of Rochus Dedler, the Village schoolmaster who wrote the Haydnesque music for the Play and died in 1821, is outside the north door of the Parish Church, and that of Joseph Daisenberger who wrote the words is outside the south door. The names on the graves in the churchyard show that the same families have lived in the Village for generations as are involved in the Passion Play now.

Information

The times of the main Sunday Mass, with choir and orchestra, in non-Play years is normally 9.30 a.m. For other services consult the notices at the church, or on the internet at http://www.pfarrverband-oberammergau.de/

Click on <St Peter und Paul> for the page about the church in Oberammergau, with times of meetings and concerts; then click on <Gottesdienste> for the times of all the services.

In the months during which the Passion Play is performed, the service times will be changed, and because of the change in performance times to afternoon and evening in 2010, nobody is quite sure what they will be, though we are told there will be a Mass on Sundays at 8 a.m. At present the notices and the internet site are all in German.

Katholisches Pfarramt, Herkulan-Schwaigergasse 5, D-82487
Oberammergau, Germany. Office hours Mon.–Fri. 9 a.m.
to 12 noon, Thu. 3 – 5 p.m. Tel. +49 (0) 8822 92290, Fax
922999.
Internet: www.pfarrverband-oberammergau.de
E-mail: Oberammergau-katholisch@web.de

THE LUTHERAN CHURCH

The other church in Oberammergau is the Evangelical-
Lutheran Church.

There are quite large numbers of German Protestants
throughout Bavaria, and the Lutheran Pastor shares with the
Catholic Priest in saying prayers with the cast of the Passion
Play before each performance.

The Lutheran church building, close to the Passion Play
Theatre, is dedicated to the Cross, and they have a custom of
inviting visitors to write their worries on slips of paper and
leave them pinned to a large wooden cross inside. Underneath
the church is a hall where 'open house' is held throughout the
Play season.

Because there are so many American Lutheran visitors, the
Lutheran Church in Oberammergau brings in additional bi-
lingual pastors in Passion Play years, who conduct their services in both English and German. It is a peaceful place for
quiet meditation.

Information

Services in the Lutheran Church are normally held on Sundays
and Festivals at 10 a.m. For other services consult the notices
at the church, or on the internet at www.oberammergau-
evangelisch.de/

At present the notices and the internet site are all in German.
Click on <Gottesdienste> or <Aktuelles> for the times of all the
services. Click on <Passionsspiel2010> for details of the activities in the months during which the Passion Play is performed,
though this page is still incomplete. There are usually English-

speaking German pastors, services to reflect on the message of the play, and an opportunity to socialize with local people and with other playgoers in the room underneath the church, to which all are welcome.

Theaterstraße 10, D-82487 Oberammergau. Tel. +49 (0) 8822 93030, Fax 93031. Office hours Tuesday and Thursday 4–6 p.m. Internet: www.oberammergau-evangelisch.de/index01.htm and www.passion-evangelisch.de/index01.htm E-mail: info@oberammergau-evangelisch.de

BRITISH MINISTERS

For the past 120 years, there have been British clergy and ministers resident in Oberammergau throughout the Passion Play season, thanks to the generosity of the Diocese in Europe and a number of tour operators. But with the change of the performance times and all that follows from that, it has not so far been possible to arrange this for 2010. However, visitors from English-speaking countries are welcomed to join in the worship and social activities at the Roman Catholic and Lutheran churches in the Village, and many of the German ministers and people in the congregation speak English. Any minister or priest wishing to conduct a special service for his or her own group is advised to contact the Katholisches Pfarramt, Herkulan-Schwaigergasse 5 (see above). It is likely that the Roman Catholic Church Hall, on the corner of Herkulan-Schwaigergasse and Hillernstraße, east of the Parish Church, will be available by arrangement for this purpose.

TAKING THE EXPERIENCE HOME WITH YOU

It would be wrong to stir up false emotionalism, which has no lasting effects. For most people, however, to realize how much they are loved is a very emotional experience. Stiff-upper-lipped English gentlemen can sometimes be seen at the Passion

Judas hangs himself

Play struggling to resist the tears that other people are shedding unashamedly. But sincere emotion is what moves people to good behaviour.

The death and resurrection of Jesus:

- reveals the love of God and God's understanding of our suffering;
- sets an example of heroic courage and compassion for us to follow;
- overcomes the power of guilt;
- provides a sacrifice which, when we identify with it by faith, brings the forgiveness of our sins;

- conquers the power of sin and death and leads us to eternal life;
- brings about reconciliation, 'at-one-ment', between us and God.

Who would not be grateful to God when they realize that this is what Jesus has done? Some of those who have seen the Passion Play may have the opportunity to go into other churches on their way across Europe. It is a good custom to kneel to pray for the people who worship there, and to attend a service if possible, even if it is in a language you do not understand. As the churches now grow closer together, one of the joys of travel is to discover how much we have in common with Christians of very different traditions, and what a warm welcome we receive from them when we identify ourselves as Christians. This fills us with a fresh desire to work and pray for mutual recognition and the restoration of visible unity between the churches.

One of the joyful responses we can make to the Passion Play when we return home is a resolve to be regular in worshipping in our own church. St Paul tells us that every time we break bread together we 'proclaim the Lord's death until he comes'. We can think of every Holy Communion, Eucharist or Mass as a Passion Play in which Jesus really comes to us, and we can make our own vow, like that of the Oberammergau villagers, to receive him regularly at this 're-present-ation' of his death and resurrection. Some people tell you it would be hypocritical to go to church unless you feel like it. If I only went to church when I felt like it that wouldn't be very often! Yet if Christians do go to church when their feelings are dry or even rebellious, and when the style of worship is not to their taste, that is an act of self-sacrifice which is pleasing to God, a 'sacrifice of praise'. It is amazing how often by the end of the service, even with this attitude, the experience has turned out to be rewarding.

The villagers of Oberammergau, with their faithfulness to their vow, have something to teach us all.

GOD LOVES YOU

If I were asked to sum up the message of the Passion Play, and the reason for attending it, in three words, they would be 'God loves you.'

The death and resurrection of Jesus tell of a completely personal love: God knows you by name, knows everything about you, and values you for what makes you different from any other person in the whole of creation. He accepts you as you are, though he will give you the power to change. God loves you.

It is not a case of human beings searching for a remote and uninterested God. God created the world so as to fill it with creatures that he could love. Some of those creatures, the human ones, he made capable of returning his love. They misused the freedom to love, which God had given them, by rebelling against their creator. So God came to earth to search for them and to give his life in love for them.

The disciples did not realize this all at once. For three years they travelled the Holy Land with a man named Jesus, who loved them and told them about treating God as if he were a loving Father. He said, 'Greater love has no one than this, to lay down one's life for one's friends' (John 15.13).

Jesus could have avoided the cross, by telling lies in Gethsemane, leaving his disciples to suffer, or denying what he had taught them about a God who loves sinners. Instead he willingly sacrificed his life to save them. The disciples realized at last that the love they saw in Jesus reveals the self-sacrificing love of God.

There is an element of risk involved in making anything. It might not do what it is intended for, it might not work properly. All creative activity involves risk, and concentration on making it right. Bringing up children is also a creative activity. Parents give their children increasing freedom to make their own choices. This involves risk, and great pain when they go wrong.

This gives us an insight into the heart of God the Father. God took the risk of making human beings free, aware that we would not, at first, be loving and kind as he intended us to be. God accepted the pain that this would bring him, and set about setting us straight. The cross reveals the eternal pain in the heart of God, as he struggles to create people who will respond to his love.

On the Laber mountain above Oberammergau, the paragliders jump off the mountainside, trusting the power of the invisible air to support them. We cannot see the love of God, though on the Cross we can see its effects. Not until we have taken the leap of faith involved in giving God complete control of our lives can we know that God will support us, and unstintingly give us his love through all eternity.

Peter regrets betraying Jesus

Appendices

BIBLE READINGS

Predictions of the Passion

Isaiah 52.13 – 53.12

See, my servant shall prosper; he shall be exalted and lifted up, and shall be very high. Just as there were many who were astonished at him – so marred was his appearance, beyond human semblance, and his form beyond that of mortals – so he shall startle many nations; kings shall shut their mouths because of him; for that which had not been told them they shall see, and that which they had not heard they shall contemplate.

Who has believed what we have heard? And to whom has the arm of the LORD been revealed? For he grew up before him like a young plant, and like a root out of dry ground; he had no form or majesty that we should look at him, nothing in his appearance that we should desire him.

He was despised and rejected by others; a man of suffering and acquainted with infirmity; and as one from whom others hide their faces he was despised, and we held him of no account. Surely he has borne our infirmities and carried our diseases; yet we accounted him stricken, struck down by God, and afflicted. But he was wounded for our transgressions, crushed for our iniquities; upon him was the punishment that made us whole, and by his bruises we are healed.

All we like sheep have gone astray; we have all turned to our own way, and the LORD has laid on him the iniquity of us all. He was oppressed, and he was afflicted, yet he did not open his mouth; like a lamb that is led to the slaughter, and like a sheep that before its shearers is silent, so he did not open his mouth. By a perversion of justice he was taken away. Who could have imagined his future? For he was cut off from the land of the living, stricken for the transgression of my people. They made his grave with the wicked and his tomb with the rich, although he had done no violence, and there was no deceit in his mouth. Yet it was the will of the LORD to crush him with pain. When you make his life an offering for sin, he shall see his offspring, and shall prolong his days; through him the will of the LORD shall prosper. Out of his anguish he shall see light; he shall find satisfaction through his knowledge. The righteous one, my servant, shall make many righteous, and he shall bear their iniquities.

Therefore I will allot him a portion with the great, and he shall divide the spoil with the strong; because he poured out himself to death, and was numbered with the transgressors; yet he bore the sin of many, and made intercession for the transgressors.

Mark 10.32–45

They were on the road, going up to Jerusalem, and Jesus was walking ahead of them; they were amazed, and those who followed were afraid. He took the twelve aside again and began to tell them what was to happen to him, saying, 'See, we are going up to Jerusalem, and the Son of Man will be handed over to the chief priests and the scribes, and they will condemn him to death; then they will hand him over to the Gentiles; they will mock him, and spit upon him, and flog him, and kill him; and after three days he will rise again.'

James and John, the sons of Zebedee, came forward to him and said to him, 'Teacher, we want you to do for us whatever we ask of you.' And he said to them, 'What is it you want me to do for you?' And they said to him, 'Grant us to sit, one at your right hand and one at your left, in your glory.' But Jesus said to them, 'You do not know what you are asking. Are you able to drink the cup that I drink, or be baptized with the baptism that I am baptized with?' They replied, 'We are able.' Then Jesus said to them, 'The cup that I drink you will drink;

and with the baptism with which I am baptized, you will be baptized; but to sit at my right hand or at my left is not mine to grant, but it is for those for whom it has been prepared.'

When the ten heard this, they began to be angry with James and John. So Jesus called them and said to them, 'You know that among the Gentiles those whom they recognize as their rulers lord it over them, and their great ones are tyrants over them. But it is not so among you; but whoever wishes to become great among you must be your servant, and whoever wishes to be first among you must be slave of all. For the Son of Man came not to be served but to serve, and to give his life a ransom for many.'

The Triumphal Entry

Matthew 21.1–17

When they had come near Jerusalem and had reached Bethphage, at the Mount of Olives, Jesus sent two disciples, saying to them, 'Go into the village ahead of you, and immediately you will find a donkey tied, and a colt with her; untie them and bring them to me. If anyone says anything to you, just say this, "The Lord needs them." And he will send them immediately.' This took place to fulfil what had been spoken through the prophet, saying, 'Tell the daughter of Zion, Look, your king is coming to you, humble, and mounted on a donkey, and on a colt, the foal of a donkey.' The disciples went and did as Jesus had directed them; they brought the donkey and the colt, and put their cloaks on them, and he sat on them. A very large crowd spread their cloaks on the road, and others cut branches from the trees and spread them on the road. The crowds that went ahead of him and that followed were shouting, 'Hosanna to the Son of David! Blessed is the one who comes in the name of the Lord! Hosanna in the highest heaven!' When he entered Jerusalem, the whole city was in turmoil, asking, 'Who is this?' The crowds were saying, 'This is the prophet Jesus from Nazareth in Galilee.'

Then Jesus entered the temple and drove out all who were selling and buying in the temple, and he overturned the tables of the money-changers and the seats of those who sold doves. He said to them, 'It is written, "My house shall be called a house of prayer"; but you are making it a den of robbers.'

The blind and the lame came to him in the temple, and he cured them. But when the chief priests and the scribes saw the amazing things that he did, and heard the children crying out in the temple, 'Hosanna to the Son of David,' they became angry and said to him, 'Do you hear what these are saying?' Jesus said to them, 'Yes; have you never read, "Out of the mouths of infants and nursing babies you have prepared praise for yourself"?' He left them, went out of the city to Bethany, and spent the night there.

The Last Supper

Matthew 26.17–29

On the first day of Unleavened Bread the disciples came to Jesus, saying, 'Where do you want us to make the preparations for you to eat the Passover?' He said, 'Go into the city to a certain man, and say to him, "The Teacher says, My time is near; I will keep the Passover at your house with my disciples."' So the disciples did as Jesus had directed them, and they prepared the Passover meal.

When it was evening, he took his place with the twelve; and while they were eating, he said, 'Truly I tell you, one of you will betray me.' And they became greatly distressed and began to say to him one after another, 'Surely not I, Lord?' He answered, 'The one who has dipped his hand into the bowl with me will betray me. The Son of Man goes as it is written of him, but woe to that one by whom the Son of Man is betrayed! It would have been better for that one not to have been born.' Judas, who betrayed him, said, 'Surely not I, Rabbi?' He replied, 'You have said so.'

While they were eating, Jesus took a loaf of bread, and after blessing it he broke it, gave it to the disciples, and said, 'Take, eat; this is my body.' Then he took a cup, and after giving thanks he gave it to them, saying, 'Drink from it, all of you; for this is my blood of the covenant, which is poured out for many for the forgiveness of sins. I tell you, I will never again drink of this fruit of the vine until that day when I drink it new with you in my Father's kingdom.'

John 13.1–20

Now before the festival of the Passover, Jesus knew that his hour had come to depart from this world and go to the Father. Having loved his own who were in the world, he loved them to the end. The devil had already put it into the heart of Judas son of Simon Iscariot to betray him. And during supper Jesus, knowing that the Father had given all things into his hands, and that he had come from God and was going to God, got up from the table, took off his outer robe, and tied a towel around himself. Then he poured water into a basin and began to wash the disciples' feet and to wipe them with the towel that was tied around him. He came to Simon Peter, who said to him, 'Lord, are you going to wash my feet?' Jesus answered, 'You do not know now what I am doing, but later you will understand.' Peter said to him, 'You will never wash my feet.' Jesus answered, 'Unless I wash you, you have no share with me.' Simon Peter said to him, 'Lord, not my feet only but also my hands and my head!' Jesus said to him, 'One who has bathed does not need to wash, except for the feet, but is entirely clean. And you are clean, though not all of you.' For he knew who was to betray him; for this reason he said, 'Not all of you are clean.'

After he had washed their feet, had put on his robe, and had returned to the table, he said to them, 'Do you know what I have done to you? You call me Teacher and Lord – and you are right, for that is what I am. So if I, your Lord and Teacher, have washed your feet, you also ought to wash one another's feet. For I have set you an example, that you also should do as I have done to you. Very truly, I tell you, servants are not greater than their master, nor are messengers greater than the one who sent them. If you know these things, you are blessed if you do them. I am not speaking of all of you; I know whom I have chosen. But it is to fulfil the scripture, "The one who ate my bread has lifted his heel against me." I tell you this now, before it occurs, so that when it does occur, you may believe that I am he. Very truly, I tell you, whoever receives one whom I send receives me; and whoever receives me receives him who sent me.'

Gethsemane

Mark 14.32–42

They went to a place called Gethsemane; and he said to his disciples, 'Sit here while I pray.' He took with him Peter and James and John, and began to be distressed and agitated. And he said to them, 'I am deeply grieved, even to death; remain here, and keep awake.' And going a little farther, he threw himself on the ground and prayed that, if it were possible, the hour might pass from him. He said, 'Abba, Father, for you all things are possible; remove this cup from me; yet, not what I want, but what you want.' He came and found them sleeping; and he said to Peter, 'Simon, are you asleep? Could you not keep awake one hour? Keep awake and pray that you may not come into the time of trial; the spirit indeed is willing, but the flesh is weak.' And again he went away and prayed, saying the same words. And once more he came and found them sleeping, for their eyes were very heavy; and they did not know what to say to him. He came a third time and said to them, 'Are you still sleeping and taking your rest? Enough! The hour has come; the Son of Man is betrayed into the hands of sinners. Get up, let us be going. See, my betrayer is at hand.'

Matthew 26.47–56

While Jesus was still speaking, Judas, one of the twelve, arrived; with him was a large crowd with swords and clubs, from the chief priests and the elders of the people. Now the betrayer had given them a sign, saying, 'The one I will kiss is the man; arrest him.' At once he came up to Jesus and said, 'Greetings, Rabbi!' and kissed him. Jesus said to him, 'Friend, do what you are here to do.' Then they came and laid hands on Jesus and arrested him. Suddenly, one of those with Jesus put his hand on his sword, drew it, and struck the slave of the high priest, cutting off his ear. Then Jesus said to him, 'Put your sword back into its place; for all who take the sword will perish by the sword. Do you think that I cannot appeal to my Father, and he will at once send me more than twelve legions of angels? But how then would the scriptures be fulfilled, which say it must happen in this way?' At that hour Jesus said to the crowds, 'Have you come out with swords and clubs to arrest me as though I were a bandit? Day after day I sat in the temple teaching, and you did not arrest me. But all this has taken place, so that the scriptures of the prophets may be fulfilled.' Then all the disciples deserted him and fled.

The trial

Mark 14.53—15.1

They took Jesus to the high priest; and all the chief priests, the elders, and the scribes were assembled. Peter had followed him at a distance, right into the courtyard of the high priest; and he was sitting with the guards, warming himself at the fire. Now the chief priests and the whole council were looking for testimony against Jesus to put him to death; but they found none. For many gave false testimony against him, and their testimony did not agree. Some stood up and gave false testimony against him, saying, 'We heard him say, "I will destroy this temple that is made with hands, and in three days I will build another, not made with hands."' But even on this point their testimony did not agree. Then the high priest stood up before them and asked Jesus, 'Have you no answer? What is it that they testify against you?' But he was silent and did not answer. Again the high priest asked him, 'Are you the Messiah, the Son of the Blessed One?' Jesus said, 'I am; and "you will see the Son of Man seated at the right hand of the Power," and "coming with the clouds of heaven."' Then the high priest tore his clothes and said, 'Why do we still need witnesses? You have heard his blasphemy! What is your decision?' All of them condemned him as deserving death. Some began to spit on him, to blindfold him, and to strike him, saying to him, 'Prophesy!' The guards also took him over and beat him.

While Peter was below in the courtyard, one of the servant-girls of the high priest came by. When she saw Peter warming himself, she stared at him and said, 'You also were with Jesus, the man from Nazareth.' But he denied it, saying, 'I do not know or understand what you are talking about.' And he went out into the forecourt. Then the cock crowed. And the servant-girl, on seeing him, began again to say to the bystanders, 'This man is one of them.' But again he denied it. Then after a little while the bystanders again said to Peter, 'Certainly you are one of them; for you are a Galilean.' But he began to curse, and he swore an oath, 'I do not know this man you are talking about.' At that moment the cock crowed for the second time. Then Peter remembered that Jesus had said to him, 'Before the cock crows twice, you will deny me three times.' And he broke down and wept.

As soon as it was morning, the chief priests held a consultation with the elders and scribes and the whole council. They bound Jesus, led him away, and handed him over to Pilate.

John 18.28 – 19.15

Then they took Jesus from Caiaphas to Pilate's headquarters. It was early in the morning. They themselves did not enter the headquarters, so as to avoid ritual defilement and to be able to eat the Passover. So Pilate went out to them and said, 'What accusation do you bring against this man?' They answered, 'If this man were not a criminal, we would not have handed him over to you.' Pilate said to them, 'Take him yourselves and judge him according to your law.' The Jews replied, 'We are not permitted to put anyone to death.' (This was to fulfil what Jesus had said when he indicated the kind of death he was to die.)

Then Pilate entered the headquarters again, summoned Jesus, and asked him, 'Are you the King of the Jews?' Jesus answered, 'Do you ask this on your own, or did others tell you about me?' Pilate replied, 'I am not a Jew, am I? Your own nation and the chief priests have handed you over to me. What have you done?' Jesus answered, 'My kingdom is not from this world. If my kingdom were from this world, my followers would be fighting to keep me from being handed over to the Jews. But as it is, my kingdom is not from here.' Pilate asked him, 'So you are a king?' Jesus answered, 'You say that I am a king. For this I was born, and for this I came into the world, to testify to the truth. Everyone who belongs to the truth listens to my voice.' Pilate asked him, 'What is truth?'

After he had said this, he went out to the Jews again and told them, 'I find no case against him. But you have a custom that I release someone for you at the Passover. Do you want me to release for you the King of the Jews?' They shouted in reply, 'Not this man, but Barabbas!' Now Barabbas was a bandit.

Then Pilate took Jesus and had him flogged. And the soldiers wove a crown of thorns and put it on his head, and they dressed him in a purple robe. They kept coming up to him, saying, 'Hail, King of the Jews!' and striking him on the face. Pilate went out again and said to them, 'Look, I am bringing him out to you to let you know that I find no case against him.' So Jesus came out, wearing the crown of thorns and the purple robe. Pilate said to them, 'Here is the man!' When the chief priests and the police saw him, they shouted, 'Crucify him! Crucify him!' Pilate said to them, 'Take him yourselves and crucify him; I find no case against him.' The Jews answered him, 'We have a law, and according to that law he ought to die because he has claimed to be the Son of God.'

Now when Pilate heard this, he was more afraid than ever. He entered his headquarters again and asked Jesus, 'Where are you from?' But Jesus gave him no answer. Pilate therefore said to him, 'Do you refuse to speak to me? Do you not know that I have power to release you, and power to crucify you?' Jesus answered him, 'You would have no power over me unless it had been given you from above; therefore the one who handed me over to you is guilty of a greater sin.' From then on Pilate tried to release him, but the Jews cried out, 'If you release this man, you are no friend of the emperor. Everyone who claims to be a king sets himself against the emperor.'

When Pilate heard these words, he brought Jesus outside and sat on the judge's bench at a place called The Stone Pavement, or in Hebrew Gabbatha. Now it was the day of Preparation for the Passover; and it was about noon. He said to the Jews, 'Here is your King!' They cried out, 'Away with him! Away with him! Crucify him!' Pilate asked them, 'Shall I crucify your King?' The chief priests answered, 'We have no king but the emperor.'

Matthew 27.15–31

Now at the festival the governor was accustomed to release a prisoner for the crowd, anyone whom they wanted. At that time they had a notorious prisoner, called Jesus Barabbas. So after they had gathered, Pilate said to them, 'Whom do you want me to release for you, Jesus Barabbas or Jesus who is called the Messiah?' For he realized that it was out of jealousy that they had handed him over. While he was sitting on the judgment seat, his wife sent word to him, 'Have nothing to do with that innocent man, for today I have suffered a great deal because of a dream about him.' Now the chief priests and the elders persuaded the crowds to ask for Barabbas and to have Jesus killed. The governor again said to them, 'Which of the two do you want me to release for you?' And they said, 'Barabbas.' Pilate said to them, 'Then what should I do with Jesus who is called the Messiah?' All of them said, 'Let him be crucified!' Then he asked, 'Why, what evil has he done?' But they shouted all the more, 'Let him be crucified!'

So when Pilate saw that he could do nothing, but rather that a riot was beginning, he took some water and washed his hands before the crowd, saying, "I am innocent of this man's blood; see to it yourselves." Then the people as a whole answered, "His blood be on us and on our children!" So he released Barabbas for them; and after flogging Jesus, he handed him over to be crucified.

Then the soldiers of the governor took Jesus into the governor's headquarters, and they gathered the whole cohort around him. They stripped him and put a scarlet robe on him, and after twisting some thorns into a crown, they put it on his head. They put a reed in his right hand and knelt before him and mocked him, saying, 'Hail, King of the Jews!' They spat on him, and took the reed and struck him on the head. After mocking him, they stripped him of the robe and put his own clothes on him. Then they led him away to crucify him.

Luke 23.26–32

As they led Jesus away, they seized a man, Simon of Cyrene, who was coming from the country, and they laid the cross on him, and made him carry it behind Jesus. A great number of the people followed him, and among them were women who were beating their breasts and wailing for him. But Jesus turned to them and said, 'Daughters of Jerusalem, do not weep for me, but weep for yourselves and for your children. For the days are surely coming when they will say, "Blessed are the barren, and the wombs that never bore, and the breasts that never nursed." Then they will begin to say to the mountains, "Fall on us"; and to the hills, "Cover us." For if they do this when the wood is green, what will happen when it is dry?'

Two others also, who were criminals, were led away to be put to death with him.

The Crucifixion according to Matthew

Matthew 27.33–66

And when they came to a place called Golgotha (which means Place of a Skull), they offered Jesus wine to drink, mixed with gall; but when he tasted it, he would not drink it. And when they had crucified him, they divided his clothes among them-selves by casting lots; then they sat down there and kept watch over him. Over his head they put the charge against him, which read, 'This is Jesus, the King of the Jews.'

Then two bandits were crucified with him, one on his right and one on his left. Those who passed by derided him, shaking their heads and saying, 'You who would destroy the temple and build it in three days, save yourself! If you are the Son of God, come down from the cross.' In the same way the chief priests also, along with the scribes and elders, were mocking him, saying, 'He saved others; he cannot save himself. He is the King of Israel; let him come down from the cross now, and we will believe in him. He trusts in God; let God deliver him now, if he wants to; for he said, "I am God's Son."' The bandits who were crucified with him also taunted him in the same way.

From noon on, darkness came over the whole land until three in the afternoon. And about three o'clock Jesus cried with a loud voice, 'Eli, Eli, lema sabachthani?' that is, 'My God, my God, why have you forsaken me?' When some of the bystanders heard it, they said, 'This man is calling for Elijah.' At once one of them ran and got a sponge, filled it with sour wine, put it on a stick, and gave it to him to drink. But the others said, 'Wait, let us see whether Elijah will come to save him.' Then Jesus cried again with a loud voice and breathed his last. At that moment the curtain of the temple was torn in two, from top to bottom. The earth shook, and the rocks were split. The tombs also were opened, and many bodies of the saints who had fallen asleep were raised. After his resurrection they came out of the tombs and entered the holy city and appeared to many. Now when the centurion and those with him, who were keeping watch over Jesus, saw the earthquake and what took place, they were terrified and said, 'Truly this man was God's Son!'

Many women were also there, looking on from a distance; they had followed Jesus from Galilee and had provided for him. Among them were Mary Magdalene, and Mary the mother of James and Joseph, and the mother of the sons of Zebedee.

When it was evening, there came a rich man from Arimathea, named Joseph, who was also a disciple of Jesus. He went to Pilate and asked for the body of Jesus; then Pilate ordered it to be given to him. So Joseph took the body and wrapped it in a clean linen cloth and laid it in his own new tomb, which he had hewn in the rock. He then rolled a great stone to the door of the tomb and went away. Mary Magdalene and the other Mary were there, sitting opposite the tomb.

The next day, that is, after the day of Preparation, the chief priests and the Pharisees gathered before Pilate and said, 'Sir, we remember what that impostor said while he was still alive, "After three days I will rise again." Therefore command that the tomb be made secure until the third day; otherwise his disciples may go and steal him away, and tell the people, "He has been raised from the dead", and the last deception would be worse than the first.' Pilate said to them, 'You have a guard of soldiers; go, make it as secure as you can.' So they went with the guard and made the tomb secure by sealing the stone.

The Crucifixion according to Mark

Mark 15.22–47

Then they brought Jesus to the place called Golgotha (which means the place of a skull). And they offered him wine mixed with myrrh; but he did not take it. And they crucified him, and divided his clothes among them, casting lots to decide what each should take. It was nine o'clock in the morning when they crucified him. The inscription of the charge against him read, 'The King of the Jews.' And with him they crucified two bandits, one on his right and one on his left. Those who passed by derided him, shaking their heads and saying, 'Aha! You who would destroy the temple and build it in three days, save yourself, and come down from the cross!' In the same way the chief priests, along with the scribes, were also mocking him among themselves and saying, 'He saved others; he cannot save himself. Let the Messiah, the King of Israel, come down from the cross now, so that we may see and believe.' Those who were crucified with him also taunted him.

When it was noon, darkness came over the whole land until three in the afternoon. At three o'clock Jesus cried out with a loud voice, 'Eloi, Eloi, lema sabachthani?' which means, 'My God, my God, why have you forsaken me?' When some of the bystanders heard it, they said, 'Listen, he is calling for Elijah.' And someone ran, filled a sponge with sour wine, put it on a stick, and gave it to him to drink, saying, 'Wait, let us see whether Elijah will come to take him down.' Then Jesus gave a loud cry and breathed his last. And the curtain of the temple was torn in two, from top to bottom. Now when the centurion, who stood facing him, saw that in this way he breathed his last, he said, 'Truly this man was God's Son!'

There were also women looking on from a distance; among them were Mary Magdalene, and Mary the mother of James the younger and of Joses, and Salome. These used to follow him and provided for him when he was in Galilee; and there were many other women who had come up with him to Jerusalem.

When evening had come, and since it was the day of Preparation, that is, the day before the sabbath, Joseph of Arimathea, a respected member of the council, who was also himself waiting expectantly for the kingdom of God, went boldly to Pilate and asked for the body of Jesus. Then Pilate wondered if he were already dead; and summoning the centurion, he asked him whether he had been dead for some time. When he learned from the centurion that he was dead, he granted the body to Joseph. Then Joseph bought a linen cloth, and taking down the body, wrapped it in the linen cloth, and laid it in a tomb that had been hewn out of the rock. He then rolled a stone against the door of the tomb. Mary Magdalene and Mary the mother of Joses saw where the body was laid.

The Crucifixion according to Luke

Luke 23.33–56

When they came to the place that is called The Skull, they crucified Jesus there with the criminals, one on his right and one on his left. Then Jesus said, 'Father, forgive them; for they do not know what they are doing.' And they cast lots to divide his clothing. And the people stood by, watching; but the leaders scoffed at him, saying, 'He saved others; let him save himself if he is the Messiah of God, his chosen one!' The soldiers also mocked him, coming up and offering him sour wine, and saying, 'If you are the King of the Jews, save yourself!' There was also an inscription over him, 'This is the King of the Jews.' One of the criminals who were hanged there kept deriding him and saying, 'Are you not the Messiah? Save yourself and us!' But the other rebuked him, saying, 'Do you not fear God, since you are under the same sentence of condemnation? And we indeed have been condemned justly, for we are getting what we deserve for our deeds, but this man has done nothing wrong.' Then he said, 'Jesus, remember me when you come into your kingdom.' He replied, 'Truly I tell you, today you will be with me in Paradise.'

It was now about noon, and darkness came over the whole land until three in the afternoon, while the sun's light failed; and the curtain of the temple was torn in two. Then Jesus, crying with a loud voice, said, 'Father, into your hands I commend my spirit.' Having said this, he breathed his last. When the centurion saw what had taken place, he praised God and said, 'Certainly this man was innocent.' And when all the crowds who had gathered there for this spectacle saw what had taken place, they returned home, beating their breasts. But all his acquaintances, including the women who had followed him from Galilee, stood at a distance, watching these things.

Now there was a good and righteous man named Joseph, who, though a member of the council, had not agreed to their plan and action. He came from the Jewish town of Arimathea, and he was waiting expectantly for the kingdom of God. This man went to Pilate and asked for the body of Jesus. Then he took it down, wrapped it in a linen cloth, and laid it in a rock-hewn tomb where no one had ever been laid. It was the day of Preparation, and the sabbath was beginning. The women who had come with him from Galilee followed, and they saw the tomb and how his body was laid. Then they returned, and prepared spices and ointments.

On the sabbath they rested according to the commandment.

The Crucifixion according to John

John 19.16b–42

So they took Jesus; and carrying the cross by himself, he went out to what is called The Place of the Skull, which in Hebrew is called Golgotha. There they crucified him, and with him two others, one on either side, with Jesus between them. Pilate also had an inscription written and put on the cross. It read, 'Jesus of Nazareth, the King of the Jews.' Many of the Jews read this inscription, because the place where Jesus was crucified was near the city; and it was written in Hebrew, in Latin, and in Greek. Then the chief priests of the Jews said to Pilate, 'Do not write, "The King of the Jews," but, "This man said, I am King of the Jews."' Pilate answered, 'What I have written I have written.' When the soldiers had crucified Jesus, they took his clothes and divided them into four parts, one for each soldier. They also took his tunic; now the tunic was seamless, woven in one piece from the top. So they said to one another, 'Let us not tear it, but cast lots for it to see who will get it.' This was to fulfil what the scripture says, 'They divided my clothes among themselves, and for my clothing they cast lots.' And that is what the soldiers did.

Meanwhile, standing near the cross of Jesus were his mother, and his mother's sister, Mary the wife of Clopas, and Mary Magdalene. When Jesus saw his mother and the disciple whom he loved standing beside her, he said to his mother, 'Woman, here is your son.' Then he said to the disciple, 'Here is your mother.' And from that hour the disciple took her into his own home.

After this, when Jesus knew that all was now finished, he said (in order to fulfil the scripture), 'I am thirsty.' A jar full of sour wine was standing there. So they put a sponge full of the wine on a branch of hyssop and held it to his mouth. When Jesus had received the wine, he said, 'It is finished.' Then he bowed his head and gave up his spirit.

Since it was the day of Preparation, the Jews did not want the bodies left on the cross during the sabbath, especially because that sabbath was a day of great solemnity. So they asked Pilate to have the legs of the crucified men broken and the bodies removed. Then the soldiers came and broke the legs of the first and of the other who had been crucified with him. But when they came to Jesus and saw that he was already dead, they did not break his legs. Instead, one of the soldiers pierced his side with a spear, and at once blood and water came out. (He who saw this has testified so that you also may believe. His testimony is true, and he knows that he tells the truth.) These things occurred so that the scripture might be fulfilled, 'None of his bones shall be broken.' And again another passage of scripture says, 'They will look on the one whom they have pierced.'

After these things, Joseph of Arimathea, who was a disciple of Jesus, though a secret one because of his fear of the Jews, asked Pilate to let him take away the body of Jesus. Pilate gave him permission; so he came and removed his body. Nicodemus, who had at first come to Jesus by night, also came, bringing a mixture of myrrh and aloes, weighing about a hundred pounds. They took the body of Jesus and wrapped it with the spices in linen cloths, according to the burial custom of the Jews. Now there was a garden in the place where he was cruci-fied, and in the garden there was a new tomb in which no one had ever been laid. And so, because it was the Jewish day of Preparation, and the tomb was nearby, they laid Jesus there.

The meaning of the cross

2 Corinthians 5.14–20

For the love of Christ urges us on, because we are convinced that one has died for all; therefore all have died. And he died for all, so that those who live might live no longer for themselves, but for him who died and was raised for them.

From now on, therefore, we regard no one from a human point of view; even though we once knew Christ from a human point of view, we know him no longer in that way. So if anyone is in Christ, there is a new creation: everything old has passed away; see, everything has become new! All this is from God, who reconciled us to himself through Christ, and has given us the ministry of reconciliation; that is, in Christ God was reconciling the world to himself, not counting their trespasses against them, and entrusting the message of recon-ciliation to us. So we are ambassadors for Christ, since God is making his appeal through us; we entreat you on behalf of Christ, be reconciled to God.

John 12.23–25

Jesus said, 'The hour has come for the Son of Man to be glorified. Very truly, I tell you, unless a grain of wheat falls into the earth and dies, it remains just a single grain; but if it dies, it bears much fruit. Those who love their life lose it, and those who hate their life in this world will keep it for eternal life.'

Resurrection and triumph

Luke 24.1–35

On the first day of the week, at early dawn, they came to the tomb, taking the spices that they had prepared. They found the stone rolled away from the tomb, but when they went in, they did not find the body. While they were perplexed about this, suddenly two men in dazzling clothes stood beside them. The women were terrified and bowed their faces to the ground, but the men said to them, 'Why do you look for the living among the dead? He is not here, but has risen. Remember how he told you, while he was still in Galilee, that the Son of Man must be handed over to sinners, and be crucified, and on the third day rise again.' Then they remembered his words, and returning from the tomb, they told all this to the eleven and to all the rest. Now it was Mary Magdalene, Joanna, Mary the mother of James, and the other women with them who told this to the apostles. But these words seemed to them an idle tale, and they did not believe them. But Peter got up and ran to the tomb; stooping and looking in, he saw the linen cloths by themselves; then he went home, amazed at what had happened.

Now on that same day two of them were going to a village called Emmaus, about seven miles from Jerusalem, and talking with each other about all these things that had happened. While they were talking and discussing, Jesus himself came near and went with them, but their eyes were kept from recognizing him. And he said to them, 'What are you discussing with each other while you walk along?' They stood still, looking sad. Then one of them, whose name was Cleopas, answered him, 'Are you the only stranger in Jerusalem who does not know the things that have taken place there in these days?' He asked them, 'What things?' They replied, 'The things about Jesus of Nazareth, who was a prophet mighty in deed and word before God and all the people, and how our chief priests and leaders handed him over to be condemned to death and crucified him. But we had hoped that he was the one to redeem Israel. Yes, and besides all this, it is now the third day since these things took place. Moreover, some women of our group astounded us. They were at the tomb early this morning, and when they did not find his body there, they came back and told us that they had indeed seen a vision of angels who said that he was alive. Some of those who were with us went to the tomb and found it just as the women had said; but they did not see him.' Then he said to them, 'Oh, how foolish you are, and how slow of heart to believe all that the prophets have declared! Was it not necessary that the Messiah should suffer these things and then enter into his glory?' Then beginning with Moses and all the prophets, he interpreted to them the things about himself in all the scriptures.

As they came near the village to which they were going, he walked ahead as if he were going on. But they urged him strongly, saying, 'Stay with us, because it is almost evening and the day is now nearly over.' So he went in to stay with them. When he was at the table with them, he took bread, blessed and broke it, and gave it to them. Then their eyes were opened, and they recognized him; and he vanished from their sight. They said to each other, 'Were not our hearts burning within us while he was talking to us on the road, while he was opening the scriptures to us?' That same hour they got up and returned to Jerusalem; and they found the eleven and their companions gathered together. They were saying, 'The Lord has risen indeed, and he has appeared to Simon!' Then they told what had happened on the road, and how he had been made known to them in the breaking of the bread.

John 20

Early on the first day of the week, while it was still dark, Mary Magdalene came to the tomb and saw that the stone had been removed from the tomb. So she ran and went to Simon Peter and the other disciple, the one whom Jesus loved, and said to them, 'They have taken the Lord out of the tomb, and we do not know where they have laid him.' Then Peter and the other disciple set out and went towards the tomb. The two were running together, but the other disciple outran Peter and reached the tomb first. He bent down to look in and saw the linen wrappings lying there, but he did not go in. Then Simon Peter came, following him, and went into the tomb. He saw the linen wrappings lying there, and the cloth that had been on Jesus' head, not lying with the linen wrappings but rolled up in a place by itself. Then the other disciple, who reached the tomb first, also went in, and he saw and believed; for as yet they did not understand the scripture, that he must rise from the dead. Then the disciples returned to their homes.

But Mary stood weeping outside the tomb. As she wept, she bent over to look into the tomb; and she saw two angels in white, sitting where the body of Jesus had been lying, one at the head and the other at the feet. They said to her, 'Woman, why are you weeping?' She said to them, 'They have taken away my Lord, and I do not know where they have laid him.' When she had said this, she turned round and saw Jesus standing there, but she did not know that it was Jesus. Jesus said to her, 'Woman, why are you weeping? For whom are you looking?' Supposing him to be the gardener, she said to him, 'Sir, if you have carried him away, tell me where you have laid him, and I will take him away.' Jesus said to her, 'Mary!' She turned and said to him in Hebrew, 'Rabbouni!' (which means Teacher). Jesus said to her, 'Do not hold on to me, because I have not yet ascended to the Father. But go to my brothers and say to them, "I am ascending to my Father and your Father, to my God and your God."' Mary Magdalene went and announced to the disciples, 'I have seen the Lord'; and she told them that he had said these things to her.

When it was evening on that day, the first day of the week, and the doors of the house where the disciples had met were locked for fear of the Jews, Jesus came and stood among them and said, 'Peace be with you.' After he said this, he showed them his hands and his side. Then the disciples rejoiced when they saw the Lord. Jesus said to them again, 'Peace be with you. As the Father has sent me, so I send you.' When he had said this, he breathed on them and said to them, 'Receive the Holy Spirit. If you forgive the sins of any, they are forgiven them; if you retain the sins of any, they are retained.'

But Thomas (who was called the Twin), one of the twelve, was not with them when Jesus came. So the other disciples told him, 'We have seen the Lord.' But he said to them, 'Unless I see the mark of the nails in his hands, and put my finger in the mark of the nails and my hand in his side, I will not believe.'

A week later his disciples were again in the house, and Thomas was with them. Although the doors were shut, Jesus came and stood among them and said, 'Peace be with you.' Then he said to Thomas, 'Put your finger here and see my hands. Reach out your hand and put it in my side. Do not doubt but believe.' Thomas answered him, 'My Lord and my God!' Jesus said to him, 'Have you believed because you have seen me? Blessed are those who have not seen and yet have come to believe.'

Now Jesus did many other signs in the presence of his disciples, which are not written in this book. But these are written so that you may come to believe that Jesus is the Messiah, the Son of God, and that through believing you may have life in his name.

PRAYERS

Assist us mercifully with your help, O Lord God of our salvation, that we may enter with joy upon the contemplation of those mighty acts, whereby you have given us life and immortality; through Jesus Christ our Lord. Amen.

from The Gelasian Sacramentary

O Lord our God, grant us grace to desire you with our whole heart, that so desiring we may seek and find you, and so finding you, may love you, and loving you, may hate those sins from which you have redeemed us, through Jesus Christ our Lord. Amen.

St Anselm (1033–1109)

O Lord God, our heavenly Father, regard, we pray, with your divine pity the pains of all your children; and grant that the passion of our Lord and his infinite love may make fruitful for good the tribulations of the innocent, the sufferings of the sick, and the sorrows of the bereaved; through him who suffered in our flesh and died for our sake, the same your Son our Saviour Jesus Christ. Amen.

Adapted from *The Scottish Book of Common Prayer 1929*

Jesus, poor, unknown and despised, have mercy on us, and let us not be ashamed to follow you. Jesus, accused, and wrongfully condemned, teach us to bear insults patiently, and let us not seek our own glory. Jesus, crowned with thorns and hailed in derision; buffeted, overwhelmed with injuries, griefs and humiliations; Jesus, hanging on the accursed tree, bowing the head, giving up the ghost, have mercy on us, and conform our whole lives to your spirit. Amen.

Adapted from John Wesley (1703–92)

We praise you, O God, because through Christ you have given us the hope of a glorious resurrection; so that, although death comes to us all, yet we rejoice in the promise of eternal life; for to your faithful people life is changed, not taken away; and when our mortal flesh is laid aside, an everlasting dwelling place is made ready for us in heaven.

Adapted from *The Roman Missal*

Almighty God, whose most dear Son went not up to joy but first he suffered pain, and entered not into glory before he was crucified: mercifully grant that we, walking in the way of the cross, may find it none other than the way of life and peace; through Jesus Christ our Lord. Amen.

William Reed Huntingdon (1838–1909)

Lord, in your pierced hands we lay our heart;
Lord, at your pierced feet we choose our part;
Lord, in your wounded side
let us abide;
Amen.

Source unknown

We give you thanks because for our salvation Jesus was obedient even to death on the cross. The tree of shame was made the tree of glory; and where life was lost, there life has been restored.

Adapted from *The Roman Missal*

Father, you have made us all in your likeness and you love all whom you have made; suffer not our family to separate itself from you by building barriers of race or colour. As your Son our Saviour was born of a Hebrew mother, but rejoiced in the faith of a Syrian woman and of a Roman soldier, welcomed the Greeks who sought him, and suffered a man from Africa to carry his cross; so teach us to regard the members of all races as fellow heirs of the kingdom of Jesus Christ our Lord. Amen.

By courtesy of Toc H and Oliver Warner

Blessed be your name, O Jesu, Son of the most high God; blessed be the sorrow you suffered when your holy hands and feet were nailed to the tree; and blessed your love when, the fulness of pain accomplished, you gave your soul into the hands of the Father; so by your cross and precious blood redeeming all the world, all longing souls departed and the numberless unborn; for now you are alive and reign, in the glory of the eternal Trinity, God for ever and ever. Amen.

Adapted from Jeremy Taylor (1613–67)

We thank you that at your mystical supper, Son of God, you receive us as partakers; we will not speak of the mystery to your enemies; we will not let our lips touch your body with a Judas-kiss; but like the thief we will acknowledge you: Remember us when you come in your kingdom, O Jesus Christ our Lord. Amen.

Adapted from *The Liturgy of St John Chrysostom*

O Lord Jesu Christ, Son of the living God, we pray you to set your passion, cross and death between your judgement and our souls, now and in the hour of our death. Vouchsafe to grant mercy and grace to the living, rest to the dead, to your holy Church peace and concord, and to us sinners everlasting life and glory; for you are alive and reign, with the Father and the Holy Spirit, one God for ever and ever. Amen.

Horae BVM (before the fourteenth century)

Praise to you, Lord Jesus Christ, for all the benefits you have won for us, for all the pains and insults you have borne for us. Most merciful redeemer, friend and brother, may we know you more clearly, love you more dearly, and follow you more nearly, day by day. Amen.

St Richard of Chichester (1197–1253)

O Lord Jesus Christ, son of the living God, who at the evening hour didst rest in the sepulchre, and didst thereby sanctify the grave to be a bed of hope to thy people: Make us so to abound in sorrow for our sins, which were the cause of thy passion, that when our bodies lie in the dust, our souls may live with thee; who livest and reignest with the Father and the Holy Ghost, one God, world without end. Amen.

Compline

To God be glory; to the angels honour; to Satan confusion; to the cross reverence; to the Church exaltation; to the departed quickening; to the penitent acceptance; to the sick and infirm recovery and healing; and to the four quarters of the world great peace and tranquillity; and on us who are weak and sinful may the compassion and mercies of our God come and overshadow us. Amen.

Syriac prayer

YOUR PASSION PLAY HYMN BOOK

These hymns are for singing in church, on the coach, wherever two or three meet together, or individually. They are arranged with their first lines in alphabetical order.

1   *All glory, laud, and honour*
    to thee, redeemer, king,
    to whom the lips of children
    made sweet hosannas ring.

    Thou art the king of Israel,
    thou David's royal son,
    who in the Lord's name comest,
    the king and blessed one.

    The company of angels
    are praising thee on high,
    and mortal men and all things_
    created make reply.

    The people of the Hebrews
    with palms before thee went:
    our praise and prayer and anthems
    before thee we present.

    To thee before thy passion
    they sang their hymns of praise:
    to thee now high exalted
    our melody we raise.

    Thou didst accept their praises:
    accept the prayers we bring,
    who in all good delightest,
    thou good and gracious king.

                                        St Theodulph of Orleans
                                        (trans. J. M. Neale)

15 Entry into Jerusalem

16 'Drink! My blood!'

17 Arrest in Gethsemane

18 Judas is paid thirty pieces of silver

19 Herod mocks Jesus

20 Flogged

21 'Ecce Homo'

22 Pilate sentences Jesus

23 Jesus is made to carry his cross

24 Longinus pierces Jesus' side with a spear

25 Jesus is taken down from the cross

26 Pietà

27 'I am with you always'

2   *All praise, all praise, King David's Son,*
    the royal throne is yours to claim.
    Come in the name of Israel's Lord
    and bring your people their reward!
    We praise your name! We praise your name!

Hosanna! God who dwells in heaven
send you his grace for all to see!
Hosanna! Praise to him be given
both now and through eternity!
    All praise, all praise, King David's Son . . .

Hosanna! David's royal descendant,
let heaven echo with your praise!
Hosanna! On your throne resplendent
to reign for endless glorious days!
    All praise, all praise, King David's Son . . .

Oberammergau Passion Play Chorale
(trans. Michael Counsell)

3   **Alleluia! Sing to Jesus!**
    His the sceptre, his the throne;
    alleluia! His the triumph,
    his the victory alone:
    hark! The songs of peaceful Sion
    thunder like a mighty flood;
    Jesus out of every nation
    hath redeemed us by his blood.

    Alleluia! Not as orphans
    are we left in sorrow now;
    alleluia! He is near us,
    faith believes, nor questions how:
    though the cloud from sight received him,
    when the forty days were o'er,
    shall our hearts forget his promise,
    'I am with you evermore'?

Alleluia! Bread of angels,
thou on earth our food, our stay;
alleluia! Here the sinful
flee to thee from day to day:
intercessor, friend of sinners,
earth's redeemer, plead for me,
where the songs of all the sinless
sweep across the crystal sea.

Alleluia! King eternal,
thee the Lord of Lords we own;
alleluia! Born of Mary,
earth thy footstool, heaven thy throne:
thou within the veil hast entered,
robed in flesh, our great high priest;
thou on earth both priest and victim
in the Eucharistic feast.

W. Chatterton Dix

4   **A Man there lived in Galilee**
unlike all men before,
for he alone from first to last
our flesh unsullied wore;
a perfect life of perfect deeds
once to the world was shown,
that all mankind might mark his steps
and in them plant their own.

A Man there died on Calvary
above all others brave;
his fellow-men he saved and blessed,
himself he scorned to save.
No thought can gauge the weight of woe
on him, the sinless, laid;
we only know that with his blood
our ransom price was paid.

A Man there reigns in glory now,
divine, yet human still;

that human which is all divine
death sought in vain to kill.
All power is his; supreme he rules_
the realms of time and space;
yet still our human cares and needs
find in his heart a place.

S. C. Lowry (altered)

5   **Amazing grace! how sweet the sound**
that saved a wretch like me;
I once was lost, but now am found;
was blind, but now I see.

'Twas grace that taught my heart to fear,
and grace my fears relieved;
how precious did that grace appear
the hour I first believed!

Through many dangers, toils and snares
I have already come;
'tis grace that brought me safe thus far
and grace will lead me home.

The Lord has promised good to me,
his word my hope secures;
he will my shield and portion be
as long as life endures.

Yes, when this heart and flesh shall fail
and mortal life shall cease,
I shall possess within the veil
a life of joy and peace.

When we've been there a thousand years
bright shining as the sun,
we've no less days to sing God's praise
than when we first begun.

John Newton

6   **Dear Lord and Father of mankind,**
    forgive our foolish ways!
    Reclothe us in our rightful mind,
    in purer lives thy service find,
    in deeper reverence praise.

    In simple trust like theirs who heard,
    beside the Syrian sea,
    the gracious calling of the Lord,
    let us, like them, without a word
    rise up and follow thee.

    O Sabbath rest by Galilee!
    O calm of hills above,
    where Jesus knelt to share with thee
    the silence of eternity,
    interpreted by love!

    Drop thy still dews of quietness,
    till all our strivings cease;
    take from our souls the strain and stress,
    and let our ordered lives confess
    the beauty of thy peace.

    Breathe through the heats of our desire
    thy coolness and thy balm;
    let sense be dumb, let flesh retire;
    speak through the earthquake, wind and fire,
    O still small voice of calm.

                                        J. G. Whittier

7   **From heaven you came, helpless babe,**
    entered our world, your glory veiled;
    not to be served but to serve,
    and give your life that we might live.

    This is our God, the Servant King,
    he calls us now to follow him,
    to bring our lives as a daily offering
    of worship to the Servant King.

There in the garden of tears,
my heavy load he chose to bear;
his heart with sorrow was torn,
'Yet not my will but yours,' he said.

Come see his hands and his feet,
the scars that speak of sacrifice;
hands that flung stars into space
to cruel nails surrendered.

So let us learn how to serve,
and in our lives enthrone him;
each other's needs to prefer,
for it is Christ we're serving.

Graham Kendrick (© 1983 Kingsway's Thankyou Music)

8 **Give me joy in my heart, keep me praising,**
give me joy in my heart, I pray;
give me joy in my heart, keep me praising,
keep me praising till the break of day.

Sing hosanna, sing hosanna,
sing hosanna to the King of kings!
Sing hosanna, sing hosanna,
sing hosanna to the King!

Give me peace in my heart, keep me loving,
give me peace in my heart, I pray;
give me peace in my heart, keep me loving,
keep me loving till the break of day.

Give me love in my heart, keep me serving,
give me love in my heart, I pray;
give me love in my heart, keep me serving,
keep me serving till the break of day.

Traditional

9   **In the cross of Christ I glory,**
towering o'er the wrecks of time,
all the light of sacred story
gathers round its head sublime.

When the woes of life o'ertake me,
hopes deceive and fears annoy,
never shall the cross forsake me:
lo! It glows with peace and joy.

When the sun of bliss is beaming_
light and love upon my way:
from the cross the radiance streaming
adds more lustre to the day.

Bane and blessing, pain and pleasure,
by the cross are sanctified:
peace is there that knows no measure,
joys that through all time abide.

(Repeat the first verse)

John Bowring

10   **Jesus Christ is risen today, Alleluia!**
Our triumphant holy day, Alleluia!
Who did once, upon the cross, Alleluia!
Suffer to redeem our loss. Alleluia!

Hymns of praise then let us sing, Alleluia!
Unto Christ, our heavenly king, Alleluia!
Who endured the cross and grave, Alleluia!
Sinners to redeem and save. Alleluia!

But the pains that he endured, Alleluia!
Our salvation have procured; Alleluia!
Now above the sky he's king, Alleluia!
Where the angels ever sing. Alleluia!

Based on *Lyra Davidica*

11 **Let us break bread together, we are one.**
Let us break bread together, we are one.
We are one as we stand with our face to the risen Son,
oh, Lord, have mercy on us.

Let us drink wine together, we are one.
Let us drink wine together, we are one.
We are one as we stand with our face to the risen Son,
oh, Lord, have mercy on us.

Let us praise God together, we are one.
Let us praise God together, we are one.
We are one as we stand with our face to the risen Son,
oh, Lord, have mercy on us.

Source unknown

12 **Meekness and majesty,**
manhood and deity, in perfect harmony,
the man who is God.
Lord of eternity dwells in humanity,
kneels in humility and washes our feet.

O what a mystery, meekness and majesty.
Bow down and worship
for this is your God, this is your God.

Father's pure radiance, perfect in innocence,
yet learns obedience to death on a cross.
Suffering to give us life,
conquering through sacrifice,
and as they crucify prays: 'Father forgive.'

O what a mystery, meekness and majesty.
Bow down and worship
for this is your God, this is your God.

Wisdom unsearchable, God the invisible,
love indestructible in frailty appears.
Lord of infinity, stooping so tenderly,
lifts our humanity to the heights of his throne.

O what a mystery, meekness and majesty.
Bow down and worship
for this is your God, this is your God.
This is your God.

Graham Kendrick (© 1986 Kingsway's Thankyou Music)

13 **Morning glory, starlit sky,**
leaves in springtime, swallows' flight,
autumn gales, tremendous seas,
sounds and scents of summer night;

soaring music, tow'ring words,
art's perfection, scholar's truth,
joy supreme of human love,
memory's treasure, grace of youth;

open, Lord, are these, thy gifts,
gifts of love to mind and sense;
hidden is love's agony,
love's endeavour, love's expense.

Love that gives, gives ever more,
gives with zeal, with eager hands,
spares not, keeps not, all outpours,
ventures all, its all expends.

Drained is love in making full,
bound in setting others free,
poor in making many rich,
weak in giving power to be.

Therefore he who thee reveals
hangs, O Father, on that tree
helpless; and the nails and thorns
tell of what thy love must be.

Thou art God: no monarch thou,
throned in easy state to reign;
thou art God, whose arms of love
aching, spent, the world sustain.

W. H. Vanstone (© Mr J. W. Shore)

14 My song is love unknown,
my saviour's love to me,
love to the loveless shown,
that they might lovely be.
O, who am I that for my sake
my Lord should take frail flesh, and die?

He came from his blest throne,
salvation to bestow;
but men made strange, and none_
the longed-for Christ would know.
But O, my friend, my friend indeed,
who at my need his life did spend.

Sometimes they strew his way,
and his sweet praises sing;
resounding all the day_
hosannas to their king.
Then 'Crucify!' is all their breath,
and for his death they thirst and cry.

Why, what hath my Lord done?
What makes this rage and spite?
He made the lame to run,
he gave the blind their sight.
Sweet injuries! Yet they at these_
themselves displease, and 'gainst him rise.

They rise, and needs will have_
my dear Lord made away;
a murderer they save,
the prince of life they slay.
Yet cheerful he to suffering goes,
that he his foes from thence might free.

In life no house, no home,
my Lord on earth might have;
in death no friendly tomb
but what a stranger gave.
What may I say? Heav'n was his home;
but mine the tomb wherein he lay.

Here might I stay and sing
no story so divine;
never was love, dear king,
never was grief like thine!
This is my friend, in whose sweet praise_
I all my days could gladly spend.

Samuel Crossman

15   Now thank we all our God,
with heart and hands and voices,
who wondrous things hath done,
in whom his world rejoices;
who from our mother's arms
hath blessed us on our way
with countless gifts of love,
and still is ours today.

O may this bounteous God
through all our life be near us,
with ever joyful hearts
and blessed peace to cheer us;
and keep us in his grace,
and guide us when perplexed,
and free us from all ills
in this world and the next.

All praise and thanks to God_
the Father now be given,
the Son, and him who reigns_
with them in highest heaven,
the one eternal God,
whom earth and heaven adore,
for thus it was, is now,
and shall be evermore.

M. Rinkart
(trans. Catherine Winkworth)

16 **O sacred head, surrounded_**
by crown of piercing thorn!
O bleeding head, so wounded,
so shamed and put to scorn!
Death's pallid hue comes o'er thee,
the glow of life decays;
yet angel-hosts adore thee,
and tremble as they gaze.

Thy comeliness and vigour_
is withered up and gone,
and in thy wasted figure_
I see death drawing on.
O agony and dying!
O love to sinners free!
Jesu, all grace supplying,
turn thou thy face on me.

In this thy bitter passion,
good shepherd, think of me_
with thy most sweet compassion,
unworthy though I be:
beneath thy cross abiding_
for ever would I rest,
in thy dear love confiding,
and with thy presence blest.

P. Gerhardt
(trans. H. W. Baker)

17 **Praise to the holiest in the height,**
and in the depth be praise:
in all his words most wonderful,
most sure in all his ways.

O loving wisdom of our God!
When all was sin and shame,
a second Adam to the fight
and to the rescue came.

O wisest love! That flesh and blood,
which did in Adam fail,
should strive afresh against the foe,
should strive and should prevail;

and that a higher gift than grace_
should flesh and blood refine,
God's presence and his very self,
and essence all-divine.

O generous love! That he, who smote_
in man for man the foe,
the double agony in man_
for man should undergo;

and in the garden secretly,
and on the cross on high,
should teach his brethren, and inspire_
to suffer and to die.

(Repeat the first verse)

J. H. Newman

18 **Ride on! Ride on in majesty!**
Hark! All the tribes hosanna cry!
O Saviour meek, pursue thy road
with palms and scattered garments strowed.

Ride on! Ride on in majesty!
In lowly pomp ride on to die:
O Christ, thy triumphs now begin
o'er captive death and conquered sin.

Ride on! Ride on in majesty!
The wingèd squadrons of the sky
look down with sad and wondering eyes
to see the approaching sacrifice.

Ride on! Ride on in majesty!
The last and fiercest strife is nigh:

the Father on his sapphire throne
awaits his own anointed Son.

Ride on! Ride on in majesty!
In lowly pomp ride on to die;
bow thy meek head to mortal pain,
then take, O God, thy power, and reign.

H. H. Milman

19 **Thank you, Jesus, thank you, Jesus,**
thank you, Lord, for loving me.
Thank you, Jesus, thank you, Jesus,
thank you, Lord, for loving me.

You went to Calvary, and there you died for me,
thank you, Lord, for loving me.
You went to Calvary, and there you died for me,
thank you, Lord, for loving me.

You rose up from the grave, to me new life you gave,
thank you, Lord, for loving me.
You rose up from the grave, to me new life you gave,
thank you, Lord, for loving me.

Source unknown

20 **The Lord's my shepherd, I'll not want;**
he makes me down to lie_
in pastures green; he leadeth me_
the quiet waters by.

My soul he doth restore again,
and me to walk doth make_
within the paths of righteousness,
e'en for his own name's sake.

Yea, though I walk through death's dark vale,
yet will I fear none ill;
for thou art with me, and thy rod_
and staff me comfort still.

My table thou has furnishèd
in presence of my foes;
my head thou dost with oil anoint,
and my cup overflows.

Goodness and mercy all my life
shall surely follow me;
and in God's house for evermore
my dwelling-place shall be.

Source unknown

21 **There is a green hill far away,**
without a city wall,
where the dear Lord was crucified,
who died to save us all.

We may not know, we cannot tell,
what pains he had to bear,
but we believe it was for us
he hung and suffered there.

He died that we might be forgiven,
he died to make us good,
that we might go at last to heaven,
saved by his precious blood.

There was no other good enough
to pay the price of sin;
he only could unlock the gate_
of heaven, and let us in.

O dearly, dearly has he loved,
and we must love him too,
and trust in his redeeming blood,
and try his works to do.

Mrs C. F. Alexander

22 **Thine be the glory, risen, conquering Son,**
   endless is the victory thou o'er death hast won;
   angels in bright raiment rolled the stone away,
   kept the folded grave-clothes where thy body lay.

   Thine be the glory, risen, conquering Son,
   endless is the victory thou o'er death hast won.

   Lo! Jesus meets us risen from the tomb;
   lovingly he greets us, scatters fear and gloom;
   let the church with gladness hymns of triumph sing,
   for her lord now liveth, death hath lost its sting.

   No more we doubt thee, glorious prince of life;
   life is nought without thee: aid us in our strife;
   make us more than conquerors through thy deathless
      love;
   bring us safe through Jordan to thy home above.

   Edmond Budry
   (trans. R. Birch Hoyle)

23 **To God be the glory! great things he hath done!**
   So loved he the world that he gave us his son,
   who yielded his life an atonement for sin,
   and opened the life-gate that all may go in.

   Praise the Lord! Praise the Lord!
   Let the earth hear his voice!
   Praise the Lord! Praise the Lord!
   Let the people rejoice!
   O come to the Father through Jesus the Son;
   and give him the glory, great things he hath done!

   O perfect redemption, the purchase of blood!
   To every believer the promise of God;
   the vilest offender who truly believes,
   that moment from Jesus a pardon receives.

   Great things he hath taught us, great things he hath
      done,

and great our rejoicing through Jesus the Son:
but purer and higher and greater will be_
our wonder, our worship, when Jesus we see!

Frances van Alstyne
(Fanny J. Crosby)

24 **Were you there when they crucified my Lord?**
Were you there when they crucified my Lord?
Oh, sometimes it causes me to tremble, tremble, tremble;
were you there when they crucified my Lord?

Were you there when they nailed him to the tree?
Were you there when they nailed him to the tree?
Oh, sometimes it causes me to tremble, tremble, tremble;
were you there when they nailed him to the tree?

Were you there when they laid him in the tomb?
Were you there when they laid him in the tomb?
Oh, sometimes it causes me to tremble, tremble, tremble;
were you there when they laid him in the tomb?

American folk hymn

25 **When I survey the wondrous cross,**
on which the prince of glory died,
my richest gain I count but loss,
and pour contempt on all my pride.

Forbid it, Lord, that I should boast
save in the death of Christ my God;
all the vain things that charm me most,
I sacrifice them to his blood.

See from his head, his hands, his feet,
sorrow and love flow mingled down;
did e'er such love and sorrow meet,
or thorns compose so rich a crown?

Were the whole realm of nature mine,
that were a present far too small;
love so amazing, so divine,
demands my soul, my life, my all.

Isaac Watts

LEARN A PHRASE A DAY

There are many fluent English-speaking people among the populations of Germany, Austria and Switzerland. It is a sign of friendliness, however, to make some attempt to learn the German language. It can make the visitor feel at home, without overtaxing the memory, to learn a few simple phrases each day during a 14-day holiday. Here are some suggestions; ask a German speaker to demonstrate the pronunciation.

Each of the sections below follows this format:
1 English phrases.
2 German translations.
3 German pronunciation.

1. Good morning. Good evening. Good day.
2. Guten Morgen. Guten Abend. Guten Tag.
3. Gootun morgun. Gootun aabunt. Gootun taak.

Bavarian dialect forms:
1. Hello. Good bye.
2. Grüss Gott. Pfüat di Gott *(intimate)*, Pfüat eich Gott *(plural or formal)*.
3. Grüs got. Pfüert dee got, Pfüert eye-ch got *('ch' as in loch; the 'ü' (u umlaut) is half way between 'ee' and 'oo')*.

1. Where are the toilets? Men. Ladies.
2. Wo sind die Toiletten? Herren/Männer. Damen/Frauen.
3. Voh zint dee toy-lettun? Hairun/mennur. Darmun/frowun *('ow' as in 'shower')*.

1. See you soon *(literally 'Speak to you again')*. *(On the telephone:)* Speak to you soon *(literally 'Hear you again')*.
2. Auf Wiedersehen *or* Auf Wiederschauen. Auf Wiederhören.
3. Owf veedurzayun *or* Owf veedershowun. Owf veedurhörun *('ö' is almost the same vowel as in 'dirt', 'curds', etc.)*

1. How much does that cost? One, two, three, four, five, six, seven, eight, nine, ten Euros.
2. Wieviel kostet das? Eins, zwei, drei, vier, fünf, sechs, sieben, acht, neun, zehn Euro.
3. Veefeel kostut dass? Eye-nts, tsv-eye, dr-eye, feer, fünf, zeks, zeebun, archt *('ch' as in 'loch')*, noyn, tsayn Oy-roe.

1. It costs eleven, twelve, thirteen, twenty, twenty-one, thirty, a hundred and one Euros. No, it is too dear.
2. Es kostet elf, zwölf, dreizehn, zwanzig, ein und zwanzig, dreissig, ein hundert eins Euro. Nein, es ist zu teuer.
3. Ess kostut elf, tsvölf, dr-eye-tsayn, tsvantsich, eye-n oont tsvantsich, dr-eye-sich, eye-n hoondurt eye-nts Oy-roe. N-eye-n, ess ist tsoo toyur.

1. We would like two beers/three coffees with milk, please. No, no sugar, thank you.
2. Wir möchten zwei Bier/drei Kaffee mit Milch, bitte. Nein, keinen Zucker, danke.
3. Veer möchtun tsv-eye beer/dr-eye kaffay mitt milch, bittuh. N-eye-n, k-eye-nun zookur, dankuh.

1. What time is it? One o'clock, five past two, a quarter past three.
2. Wieviel Uhr ist es? Ein Uhr, fünf Minuten nach zwei, Viertel nach drei.
3. Veefeel oor isst ess? Eye-n oor, fünf minootun naach tsv-eye, feertul naach dr-eye.

1. Half past four; a quarter to six; early tomorrow; too late.
2. Halb fünf *(literally 'half five')*; Viertel vor sechs; Morgen früh; zu spät.
3. Halp fünf; feertul for zeks; morgun frü; tsoo shpät *('ä' is the vowel in 'spare').*

1. Where is there some hot water? Cold water? Iced water? Thank you very much. It's a pleasure!
2. Wo gibt es heisses Wasser? Kaltes Wasser? Eis Wasser? Danke schön! Bitte schön!
3. Voh gibt ess h-eye-sus vassur? Kaltus vassur? Eye-ss vassur? Dankuh shön! Bittuh shön!

1. What is the weather like today? It is raining hard. The sun is shining. It's going to snow.
2. Wie ist das Wetter heute? Es regnet schwer. Die Sonne scheint. Es wird schneien.
3. Vee isst dass vettur hoytur? Ess raygnut shvayr. Dee zonnuh sh-eye-nt. Ess veert shn-eye-un.

1. We need a double room with bathroom or shower. A single room.
2. Wir brauchen ein Doppelzimmer mit Bad oder Dusche. Ein Einzelzimmer.
3. Veer browchun eye-n doppultsimmur mitt baat owe-dur dooshuh. Eye-n eye-nsultsimmer.

1. Breakfast. Lunch. Dinner. A snack. Something to drink.
2. Frühstuck. Mittagessen. Abendessen. Imbiss. Etwas zu trinken.
3. Früshtook. Mitaagessun. Aabuntessun. Imbiss. Etvass tsoo trinkun.

1. Help! Danger. Forbidden. Police. Fire. Doctor. Dentist.
2. Hilfe! Gefahr. Verboten. Polizei. Feuer. Arzt. Zahnartzt.
3. Hilfuh! Guhfaar. Fair-boat-un. Pollits-eye. Foy-uh. Artst. Tsaanartst.

1. Give me medicine for my wife/my husband. Stomach ache/heart/headache.
2. Geben sie mir Medizin für meine Frau/meinen Mann. Magenschmerzen. Herz. Kopfweh.
3. Gaybun zee meer maydeetseen für m-eye-nuh frow / m-eye-nun mann. Maagunshmairtsun. Hairts. Kopfvay.

LIST OF ILLUSTRATIONS

Maps
© *John Flower 1998*
Location of Oberammergau in Europe xxiii
Oberammergau Village 6
Bavaria, with approaches to Oberammergau 13

Colour photographs by the author
© *2008 Michael Counsell*
Front cover:
Oberammergau Village from the Laber mountain

1 Oberammergau, King Ludwig's Crucifixion Group
2 Wall-painting of the taking of the vow
3 Oberammergau Lutheran Church
4 The leap of faith: Paraglider launching from the Laber mountain
5 Oberammergau Village from the Crucifixion Group
6 Woodcarving of the crucifixion and the Last Supper in the Parish Church
7 Oberammergau Parish Church
8 Inside the Parish Church at Mass
9 The crucifix in the Parish Church before which the vow was made
10 Palm Sunday procession figure in the Parish Church
11 The Pilatushaus
12 Front of the Passion Play Theatre
13 Costumes for the Roman soldiers
14 Leonhard Höldrich jun., woodcarver

Colour pictures of the Oberammergau Passion Play in 2000
Photographs by Brigitte Maria Mayer,
copyright Oberammergau Tourismus

Front cover:
The crucifixion

Black and white pictures of the Oberammergau Passion Play in 2000

Photographs by Brigitte Maria Mayer, copyright Oberammergau Tourismus

INDEX OF SCRIPTURES

INDEX OF SUBJECTS

SOURCES AND ACKNOWLEDGEMENTS

Alexander, Mrs CF (1818–1895) 86

American Folk Hymn 88

Anselm, St (1033–1109) 68

Baker, Sir HW (1821–1877) 83

Bowring, John (1792–1872) 78

Budry, Edmond (1854–1932) 87

Compline, adapted from the Sarum Breviary by Edward Willis in *The Cuddesdon Office Book 1880* 70

Counsell, Michael, translation of the Oberammergau Play Chorale © 2000 Michael Counsell 73

Crosby, Fanny J. (Alstyne, Frances van) 87

Crossman, Samuel (1624–1683) 81

Dix, W. Chatterton (1837–1898) 73

Gelasian Sacramentary (fifth century) 68

Gerhardt, P. (1607–76) 83

Horae BVM, (pre-fourteenth century) 70

Hoyle, R. Birch (1872–1939) translation © By permission of the World Student Christian Federation, 5 Route des Morillons, 1218 Grand-Saconnex, Geneva, Switzerland 87

Huntingdon, William Reed (1838–1909) 69

Kendrick, Graham, (© 1983 & 1986 Kingsway's Thankyou Music, PO Box 85, Eastbourne, East Sussex, BN23 6NW, UK; used by permission) 76, 79

Liturgy of St John Chrysostom 70

Lowry, S.C. (1855–1932) 74

Lyra Davidica (1708) altered 78

Milman, H.H. (1799–1868) 84

Neale, John Mason (1818–1866) 72

Newman, Cardinal John Henry (1801–1890) 84

Newton, John (1725–1807) 75

Oberammergau Passion Play Chorale 73

Richard of Chichester, St (1197–1253) 70

Rinkart, M. (1586–1649) 82

YOUR NOTES

(You may like to write here the contact details of your fellow-pilgrims)